ALEXANDER VIDAL

WILDS OF THE UNITED STATES

THE ANIMALS' SURVIVAL FIELD GUIDE

chronicle books·san francisco

Library of Congress Cataloging-in-Publication Data available.

ISBN 978-1-4521-8449-4

Manufactured in China.

Art direction by Jennifer Tolo Pierce.
Design by Alexander Vidal.
Typeset in DIN 1451, Whitney, and Sentinel.
The illustrations in this book were rendered digitally.

10 9 8 7 6 5 4 3 2 1

Chronicle books and gifts are available at special quantity discounts to corporations, professional associations, literacy programs, and other organizations. For details and discount information, please contact our premiums department at corporatesales@chroniclebooks.com or at 1-800-759-0190.

Chronicle Books LLC
680 Second Street
San Francisco, California 94107

Chronicle Books—we see things differently. Become part of our community at www.chroniclekids.com.

LAND ACKNOWLEDGMENT

The wild spaces described in this book are not found on a singular landmass or even within just one hemisphere. They are gathered here because they reflect the present borders of the United States of America and its territories, a wide-ranging collection of lands stewarded by Indigenous peoples since time immemorial. These lands were taken from Indigenous peoples as part of an ongoing history of settlement, displacement, war, and colonial expansion.

These wild spaces are stolen lands, and even as we appreciate their beauty, we must consider the central role their eco-systems and wildlife have played in the history of colonization. The United States has routinely terrorized and displaced Indigenous communities in an effort to take their natural resources away from them, a practice that continues today.

We must find more opportunities to return stewardship of the land to Indigenous communities and to enact environmental policies that honor and respect their knowledge.

AUTHOR'S LAND ACKNOWLEDGMENT

Wilds of the United States was written and illustrated in northeast Los Angeles, California, on the ancestral and unceded territories of the Tongva and Chumash people.

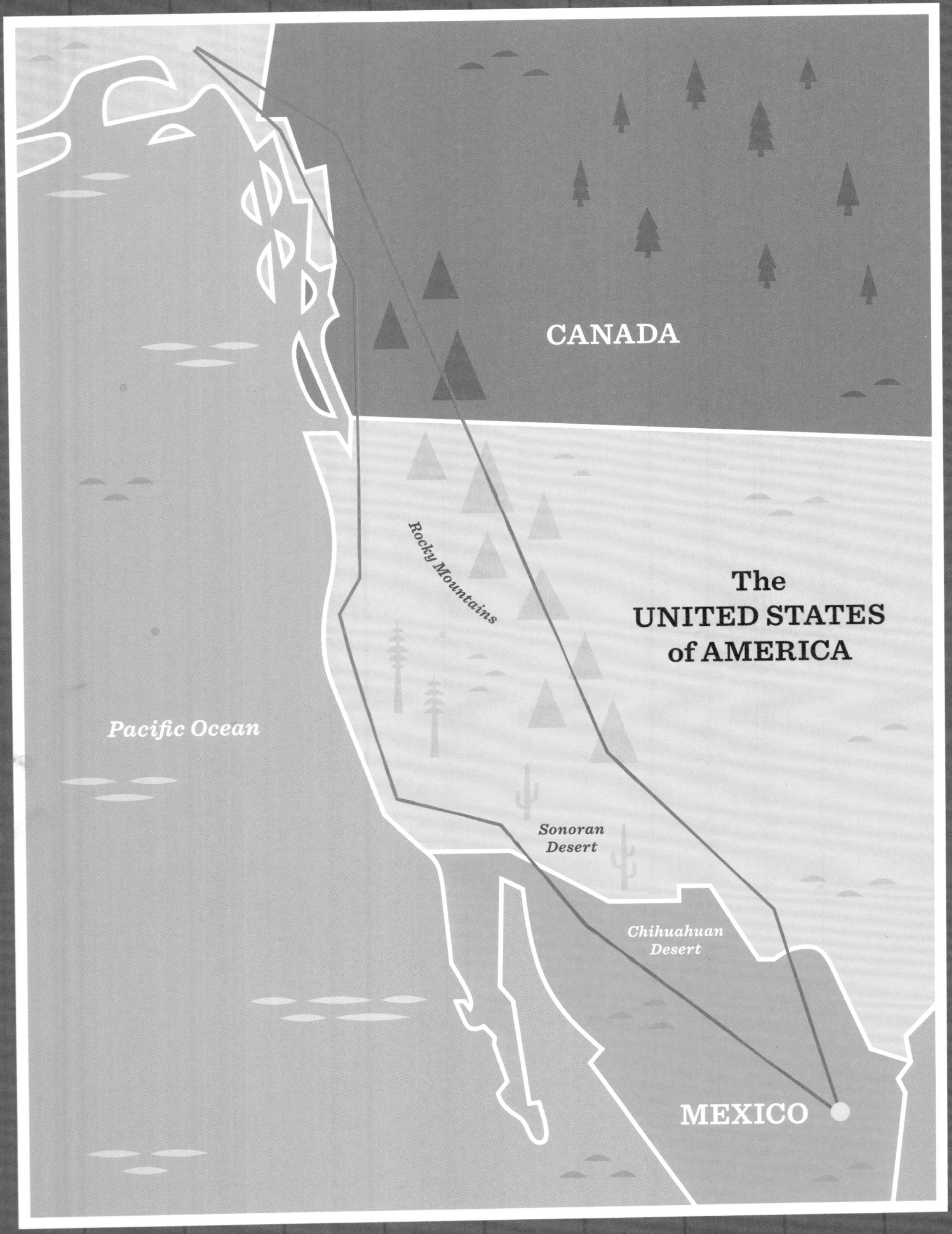

CANADA
The UNITED STATES of AMERICA
Rocky Mountains
Pacific Ocean
Sonoran Desert
Chihuahuan Desert
MEXICO

INTRODUCTION

Every year in the United States, one animal embarks on an epic voyage. As the warmth of summer begins to fade, it leaves its home in Alaska, heading south. It travels the length of the Rocky Mountains, pausing to rest and refuel in alpine meadows over 12,000 feet high. After crossing the border into Mexico and coming back again, it returns home by trekking north along the Pacific Coast. It is a round-trip journey of nearly 8,000 miles, made by a creature that weighs less than an ounce: the **rufous hummingbird**.

No matter where you are in the United States, there are animals just outside your door engaged in lives beyond imagination. Beneath the hooves of bison on the Great Plains, prairie dogs excavate elaborate underground cities, some stretching for miles. In the deserts of the west, kangaroo rats use dance moves to evade being eaten by rattlesnakes. And in southern bayous and wetlands, alligators perform prehistoric courtship rituals that long predate humankind.

This field guide tells the incredible stories of these creatures and hundreds more from throughout the United States. On a winding one-way journey across the country, we'll hike rugged mountainsides, trudge flooded swamplands, and brave the heat of expansive deserts. We'll climb towering trees, dig underground, and stay up late to see who comes out at night. We'll traverse forests, grasslands, tundra, and even vast ocean distances as we explore the incredible diversity of creatures who call the United States home.

So lace up your hiking boots and prepare yourself for adventure. Like the rufous hummingbird, we have a long journey ahead of us—**we're off to meet the neighbors.**

Join the rufous hummingbird on its voyage by flitting to page 108.

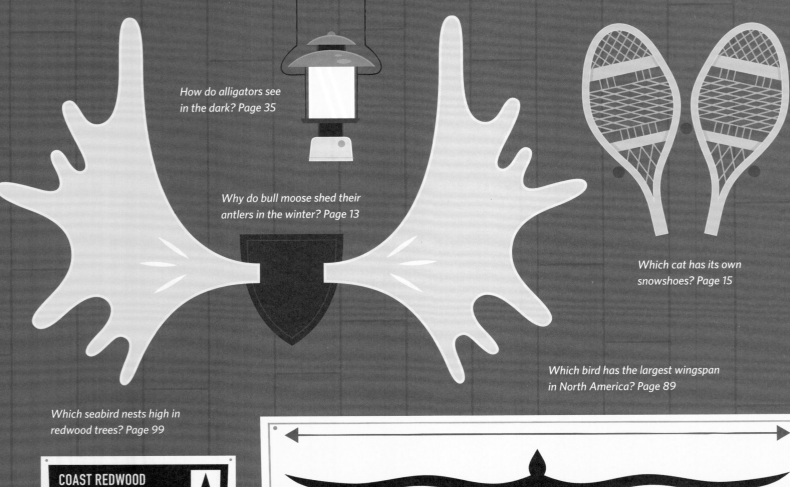

How do alligators see in the dark? Page 35

Why do bull moose shed their antlers in the winter? Page 13

Which cat has its own snowshoes? Page 15

Which bird has the largest wingspan in North America? Page 89

Which seabird nests high in redwood trees? Page 99

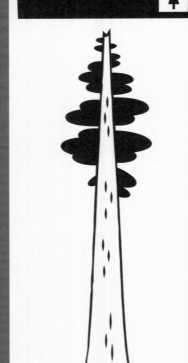

COAST REDWOOD

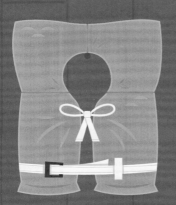

Whose strange, bugling call can be heard in the Great Smoky Mountains? Page 25

How do harlequin ducks survive raging mountain rivers? Page 64

Which reptile has a fishing lure on its tongue? Page 30

SURVIVAL SKILLS

How does an animal survive for months without rain in the Mojave or avoid predators on the open grasslands? Living in the wilds of the United States isn't easy, but America's wildlife is up for the challenge. The merit badges below appear throughout this field guide to honor and highlight the incredible skills and physical adaptations that animals use to survive.

FORAGING
Finding food is the single most important challenge that wildlife face and the first skill needed to survive.

HUNTING
Hunting requires animals to draw from a wide set of skills, including quick reflexes and cunning intelligence.

ATHLETICS
These animals survive in the wild by using their exceptional strength, speed, and agility.

FIELD SIGNALS
Animals find a variety of unique ways to send their message across the wilderness.

SHELTER
Finding or making a good shelter can protect an animal from the cold, serve as a place to store food, and give animals a place to raise their young.

UNIFORM
Being properly outfitted can help an animal survive in extreme weather, attract the attention of a mate, or protect them from predators.

PERFORMANCE
Being a good performer can help an animal avoid predators, gain social power, or attract a mate.

COMMUNITY
Going it alone can be tough, so these animals have found teamwork to be the key to their survival.

TOOLKIT
These animals have either learned how to use tools they find in their environment or they've evolved their own tools, from distinctly shaped beaks to sensitive whiskers.

NAVIGATION
These animals take advantage of different environments to survive, some traveling incredible distances throughout the United States and beyond.

SURVIVALISTS
Animals with this badge have what it takes to survive, either barely changing for millions of years or rebounding from near-extinction.

WILDERNESS EXPERTS
These incredible animals have evolved the right set of behaviors and physical adaptations to perfectly face the unique challenges of their environment.

REGIONS OF THE UNITED STATES

Covering over 3.5 million square miles and stretching from the Arctic to the tropics, the United States has one of the most varied landscapes of any country in the world. Each of these environments has something distinct to offer the animals that make their home there, but they each come with their own unique challenges as well.

START YOUR ADVENTURE HERE

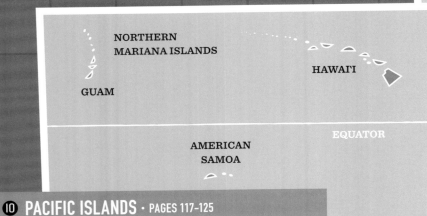

NORTHERN MARIANA ISLANDS

GUAM

HAWAI'I

EQUATOR

AMERICAN SAMOA

⑩ PACIFIC ISLANDS · PAGES 117–125

Isolated laboratories for evolution, the Pacific Islands are home to strange and incredible animals that are unlike any others in the United States.

⑨ FAR NORTH · PAGES 105–116

Stretching across Alaska, the Far North is an expansive and rugged wilderness of mountains, tundra, and icy Arctic seas.

⑧ PACIFIC COAST · PAGES 87–104

There's little boundary between land and sea on the Pacific Coast, where marine fog nurtures lush forests and predators from dry land rely on the ocean's bounty for their survival.

⑦ DESERT WEST · PAGES 71–86

Only the toughest animals survive in America's vast Desert West, where temperatures soar and months can pass without rain.

❶ EASTERN WOODLANDS · PAGES 10–20

Animals in the Eastern Woodlands must live by the rhythm of the seasons, enjoying the richness of summer and braving the challenges of winter.

❷ APPALACHIANS · PAGES 21–26

One of the oldest mountain ranges in the world, the Appalachians shelter animals in mist-cloaked valleys, dense temperate rainforests, and icy mountain streams.

❸ THE SOUTH · PAGES 27–40

Wetlands take a variety of forms in the South, from forests flooded by the Mississippi River to coastal marshlands that rise and fall with the tides.

❹ TROPIC SEAS · PAGES 41–48

The warm climate of the Tropic Seas creates a unique refuge in the United States for animals from Mexico, Central America, and the Caribbean.

❺ THE GREAT PLAINS · PAGES 49–60

In the past, America's vast grasslands provided open territory for wildlife to graze and roam, but today only fragments of these ecosystems remain.

❻ THE ROCKIES · PAGES 61–70

Stretching from Canada almost to Mexico, the Rockies are a vertical landscape of towering forests, pounding rivers, and remote alpine tundra.

PUERTO RICO

U.S. VIRGIN ISLANDS

AT FIRST LIGHT

As the sun rises over the United States, light lands first on the forested coastline of eastern Maine. The early morning light makes visible the meeting of two worlds. As the creatures of night are finishing their waking hours, the rest of the forest prepares to start its day.

Bald eagles can have a wingspan of 7 feet and can soar up to 10,000 feet high!

ATHLETICS
DIVE BOMBER

When diving to attack prey, **peregrine falcons** move at more than 200 miles per hour—faster than any other animal.

NAVIGATION
SUMMER HOUSE

Atlantic puffins spend the winter on the open ocean, returning in the summer to nest on islands off the coast of Maine.

FORAGING
VARIED VEGETARIANS

White-tailed deer feed on a wide variety of plant matter, including grasses, ferns, mushrooms, and acorns.

UNIFORM
CONTENT WARNING

The **striped skunk's** high-contrast black-and-white fur helps warn predators not to mess with it: it sprays an unpleasant liquid when attacked.

SHELTER
HOME EXPANSION

Bald eagles build a large nest out of sticks, moss, and grass. If a pair of bald eagles like their nesting site, they'll reuse it over many years, adding more material and expanding the nest each time. The largest bird's nest ever recorded belonged to a pair of bald eagles: it was over 9 feet wide, 20 feet deep, and weighed more than 2 tons!

PERFORMANCE
DRUM SOLO

To attract attention, the male **ruffed grouse** stands atop a log, puffs up his feathers, and beats his wings across his chest at a high speed, making a sound like a lawn mower starting up.

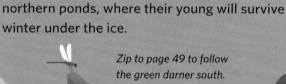

NAVIGATION
TO STAY OR TO GO

Green darners have two options as winter approaches. They can travel south, some flying as far as 900 miles. Or they can lay their eggs in northern ponds, where their young will survive winter under the ice.

Zip to page 49 to follow the green darner south.

SHELTER
LOG CABIN

American mink hunt in estuaries and waterways for fish, crustaceans, and frogs. They often build their homes in hollow logs or tree stumps, using grass or leaves to create a cozy nest.

PERFORMANCE
THE TURTLE'S TAP DANCE

To get worms to come to the surface, the **wood turtle** stomps its feet, imitating the sound of rain.

SEASONS CHANGE

In northern forests, two animals use very different strategies to survive the rhythm of seasons. One animal changes its needs to fit the environment, while the other changes the environment to fit its needs.

The largest rodents in North America, beavers can weigh up to 70 pounds.

If a beaver hears water breaking through its dam, it quickly makes repairs.

FORAGING
SEASONAL PRODUCE

As the largest species of deer in the world, **moose** need to eat a lot: up to 70 pounds of plant matter a day. In the summer, moose feed on aquatic plants and willow leaves. As the forest changes throughout the year, moose survive by altering their diet to what's available.

Blanding's turtle

ring-necked duck

hooded merganser

wood frog

common goldeneye

COMMUNITY
ENGINEER OF THE FOREST

Other than humans, no animal shapes its environment through building as much as the **North American beaver**. Beavers like to live near ponds, and when there aren't any available, they make their own. Using their front teeth, which are strengthened with iron, they chop down trees to build dams that back up creeks and streams, creating wetland habitats that many different animals rely on.

Bull moose shed their heavy antlers in the winter, helping them conserve energy. They'll regrow in the spring.

With fresh leaves and aquatic plants unavailable in the winter, moose survive by eating twigs, pine cones, and mosses.

SHELTER

A LODGE FOR ALL SEASONS

Beavers use branches, twigs, and mud to build their homes, which are called lodges. By building and maintaining their lodges throughout the summer, beavers are prepared for the harshness of winter. Beaver families spend winter inside the lodge, staying warm and hidden from predators.

Beavers store food underwater, where they're able to get to it throughout the winter, even if the pond's surface freezes over.

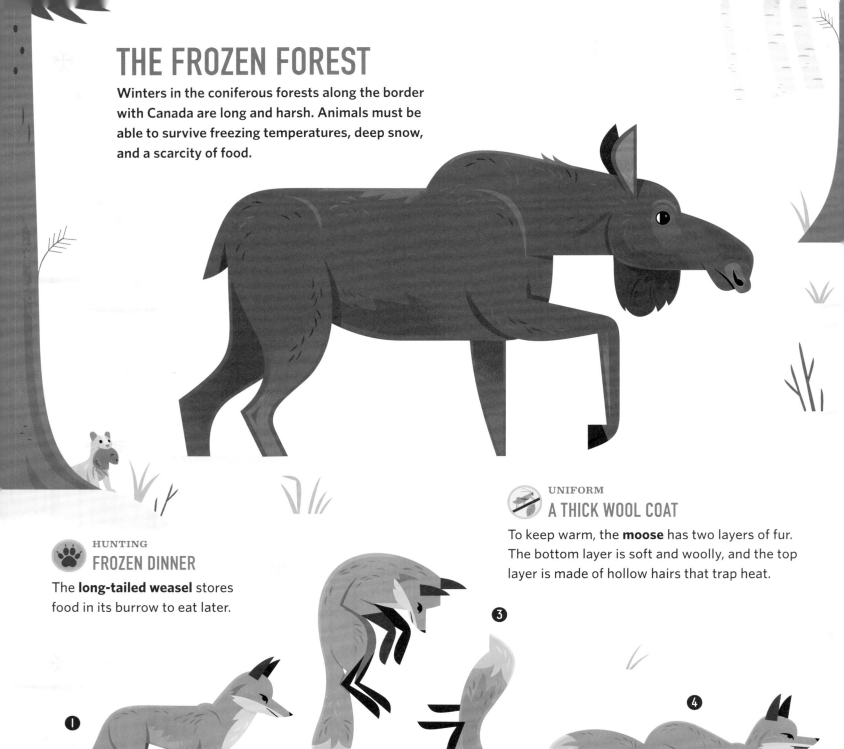

THE FROZEN FOREST

Winters in the coniferous forests along the border with Canada are long and harsh. Animals must be able to survive freezing temperatures, deep snow, and a scarcity of food.

UNIFORM
A THICK WOOL COAT

To keep warm, the **moose** has two layers of fur. The bottom layer is soft and woolly, and the top layer is made of hollow hairs that trap heat.

HUNTING
FROZEN DINNER

The **long-tailed weasel** stores food in its burrow to eat later.

HUNTING
CATCHING UNSEEN PREY

To catch voles as they travel through tunnels beneath the snow, the **red fox** puts its heightened sense of hearing to use.

1. *The fox listens for movement beneath the snow.*
2. *After taking aim, it leaps straight into the air.*
3. *Crash! It dives headfirst into the snow.*
4. *Success!*

ATHLETICS
HIGH-FLYER

The flap of skin connecting a **northern flying squirrel's** back and front paws allows it to glide between trees. This helps it stay out of the snow and avoid any predators that may be lurking below. They've been recorded gliding almost 300 feet!

TOOLKIT
THE CAT WITH SNOWSHOES

The huge paws of the **Canada lynx** work like snowshoes, spreading the lynx's weight with each step so it can walk over the surface of the snow without falling through.

UNIFORM
WARM WINTER SOCKS

The **snowshoe hare** has fur on the soles of its feet that protects it from freezing, like thick winter socks.

TOOLKIT
THE ANTIFREEZE FROG

"Antifreeze" in the **wood frog's** cells allow it to survive while it spends the winter hibernating among leaves.

SHELTER
HOME BENEATH THE SNOW

Groundhogs spend the winter hibernating in underground burrows. Many burrows have multiple entrances and rooms, and some even have more than one level.

THE GREAT LAKES

Spanning over 90,000 square miles, the Great Lakes are the largest freshwater system in the world. Wildlife find refuge on isolated islands, in shoreline forests and wetlands, and in the lakes' icy waters.

FIELD SIGNALS
YODEL AND HOOT

Common loons have different calls to announce their presence (the wavering tremolo), to locate their chicks (a quick hoot), and to claim territory (a yodel).

NAVIGATION
MONARCH MIGRATION

Every year, **monarch butterflies** travel 3,000 miles south to winter in the mountains of central Mexico. They often travel along lakeshores, roosting close together in pine and fir trees on cool autumn nights.

Float south with the monarchs to page 56 to see the role the prairie plays in their survival.

FORAGING
MEAL SUPPLEMENTS

Though they are primarily hunters, the **gray wolves** that live along the Great Lakes have been seen catching fish and eating fresh blueberries in season.

TOOLKIT
A TOUCHY NOSE

The **star-nosed mole** is nearly blind, so it uses the nerves in its unique nose to feel through wet soil and water as it hunts for worms, insects, and small fish.

FIELD SIGNALS
TAP, TAP

Mink frogs sing in chorus, making a call that sounds like a hammer striking wood.

TOOLKIT
STINK BOMBS

The **stinkpot turtle** can release a foul odor when threatened, giving it a chance to escape from predators.

NAVIGATION
DIVING DEEP

Lake trout prefer to live in cold water. They spend much of the year in shallow water near the shore, but as summer heats up, they dive over 200 feet to spend the season in icy depths.

SURVIVALISTS
THE LAKE STURGEON

Lake sturgeon have changed little in the past 150 million years, but they were almost pushed to extinction by hunting and pollution. In recent years, their population numbers have begun to rise again.

The largest fish in the Great Lakes, lake sturgeon can grow to 7 feet long and weigh over 200 pounds.

HUNTING
AMBUSH HUNTER

Northern pike lurk among the weedy lake bottoms, waiting to lunge at passing prey and grab them with their long, backward-pointing teeth.

TOOLKIT
YOUTHFUL ATTACHMENTS

In their larval stage, many species of salamanders have feathery gills to help them breathe underwater. **Mudpuppies** spend their entire lives at the bottom of lakes and ponds, so they never lose their gills.

The Mississippi River flows from the nearby Lake Itasca. Drift to page 30 to discover the strange creatures that swim in the river's waters.

TOOLKIT
FITTING THE BILL

Uniquely shaped bills allow ducks to browse wetlands for different foods.

The mallard's round-tipped bill helps it eat lots of different foods.

The serrated bill of the common merganser helps it nab fish.

The northern shoveler skims crustaceans from the water's surface with its wide, flat bill.

The wood duck's short, narrow bill allows it to grab acorns off the forest floor.

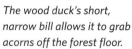

A CLEARING IN THE WOODS

In parts of the forest where trees don't block sunlight or rain, thick tangles of bushes and weeds take over. These clearings are an important habitat, offering animals a mix of open space and hiding places not found elsewhere in the forest.

HUNTING
PEST CONTROL

The **little brown bat** only weighs one-third of an ounce, but it can eat 1,000 insects in an hour.

FIELD SIGNALS
RAISING A WHITE FLAG

It can be hard for a young fawn to follow its mother through dense bushes and shrubs, so as the mother **white-tailed deer** runs, she raises her wide tail, giving her fawn a flag to follow.

White-tailed deer can leap 10 feet high and a distance of 30 feet in a single bound.

FIELD SIGNALS
AN ATTRACTIVE FRAGRANCE

To attract a mate, the female **cecropia moth** releases pheromones that can be detected over a mile away.

The largest moths in North America, cecropia moths can measure up to 7 inches.

UNIFORM
WATCHING OUT

The eye-like markings on the **polyphemus moth's** wings help scare off predators.

ATHLETICS
BEETLE BATTLE

Male **giant stag beetles** wrestle by using their enormous mandibles to flip one another over.

TOOLKIT
SATELLITE DISH

At dusk, **barn owls** fly low over fields and clearings in search of rats, mice, and voles. Their flat faces act like satellite dishes to pick up sounds, giving them the strongest ability to detect prey through sound of any animal ever recorded.

PERFORMANCE
DANCING AT DUSK

On spring evenings, male **woodcocks** take to forest clearings to perform their aerial courtship dance. They chirp, spiral into the air, and dive sharply back down to draw the attention of females.

TOOLKIT
BIG EARS

The **Townsend's big-eared bat** uses its sonar and excellent hearing to detect insects in the darkness. Its ears can be one-fourth the length of its whole body!

FIELD SIGNALS
HOME ALARMS

Male **gray catbirds** announce their territory with a loud song that can last for ten minutes. Notes in the song imitate other birds, tree frogs, and even mechanical sounds they've heard.

SHELTER
A HIDDEN NURSERY

The **eastern cottontail** builds a nest for its young in a shallow hole, disguising it to look like a patch of dead grass. They spend as little time at the nest as possible, to avoid drawing the attention of predators.

THE FOREST FLOOR

Autumn and spring are seasons of change in the woods, as seen in the many activities of animals on the forest floor. In the fall, animals prepare for the coming hardship of winter, while spring brings movement and the emergence of new life.

COMMUNITY
BIRDS OF A FEATHER

In the autumn, **wild turkeys** join together in flocks. They scratch along the forest floor, enjoying the abundance of fallen acorns.

TOOLKIT
TO-GO BAGS

Eastern chipmunks use the "pockets" in their cheeks to carry lots of seeds and nuts back to their burrow.

PERFORMANCE
PANTOMIME

Eastern gray squirrels bury thousands of acorns underground to eat throughout the winter. If they think they're being watched, they'll pretend to bury food to confuse potential acorn robbers.

SHELTER
GETTING COZY

When temperatures start to drop, **eastern box turtles** dig a shallow hole among the leaves and settle down to brumate over the winter.

UNIFORM
RED ALERT

In the fall, **eastern newt** larvae metamorphose to their juvenile phase (called efts) and leave their ponds for land. They're more vulnerable on the forest floor, so their bright red skin announces that they have toxins that make them dangerous to eat.

PERFORMANCE
STRUTTING HIS STUFF

To attract the attention of a **turkey** hen, the male (called a tom) fans out his tail feathers, lowers his wings, and struts while humming and rattling his wing feathers.

SHELTER
GROUND LEVEL

After returning from her winter migration grounds, the female **ovenbird** weaves a dome-shaped nest on the leafy forest floor.

Follow the ovenbird to her tropical wintering site on page 47.

NAVIGATION
HEADING TO THE POOL

Tiger salamanders leave their underground hiding places after the spring thaw, traveling up to half a mile to lay their eggs in vernal pools. These temporary ponds of rainwater and melting snow are free of hungry fish, making them a safer nursery for the salamander's young.

FIELD SIGNALS
SONG OF SPRING

Spring peepers spend the winter hibernating under logs or tree bark, emerging after the first thaw to begin their chorus.

COMMUNITY
MASS AWAKENING

After spending up to 17 years living underground as larvae, **periodical cicadas** emerge together at the same time as adults. They live aboveground for only a few weeks, gathering in the millions to mate and lay their eggs.

UP IN THE TREES

The Appalachians are cloaked in a blanket of green, a dense broad-leaf forest where more than 150 species of trees grow. Up in their branches, animals hunt, forage, and make their homes high above the ground.

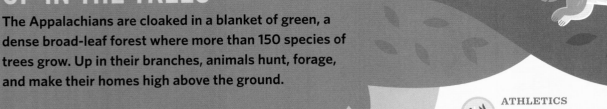

ATHLETICS
TREETOP ACROBAT

Eastern gray squirrels move nimbly among tree branches. They can leap nine feet from one branch to another and are one of only a few mammals that can climb down a tree headfirst.

UNIFORM
PAJAMAS OF INVISIBILITY

The **eastern screech owl's** mottled feathers help it camouflage with tree bark as it rests during the day.

TOOLKIT
A HANDY TAIL

The **Virginia opossum** can use its prehensile tail to climb trees, carry nesting materials, or even hang for brief periods.

WILDERNESS EXPERTS
BEARS IN THE BRANCHES

Black bears are skilled climbers, aided by their short, strong claws. They climb to find food and escape danger, and some even den over winter high up in hollow trees.

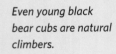

Even young black bear cubs are natural climbers.

HUNTING
BUG CATCHER

Though they feed mostly on nectar, **ruby-throated hummingbirds** will also eat insects, sometimes grabbing them out of spiderwebs.

FORAGING
CHISELED OUT

The **pileated woodpecker** carves rectangular holes in tree trunks to get to the nests of carpenter ants.

SHELTER
BUILDING MATERIALS

The forest provides a wide variety of nesting materials, which animals use in very different ways.

The eastern gray squirrel gathers twigs and leaves to make a messy nest called a drey.

Great crested flycatchers line their tree-cavity nests with snakeskin.

The bald-faced hornet queen uses wood fiber to make the paper pulp to build her nest.

The Baltimore oriole weaves a hanging nest out of grass and bark.

FORAGING
NEST INVADER

The **black rat snake** climbs trees in search of eggs.

UNIFORM
FOREST CAMOUFLAGE

To avoid being caught by predators, some insects camouflage themselves to disappear among the forest's leaves and branches.

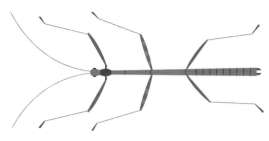

The northern walkingstick holds itself still to blend in with twigs and branches.

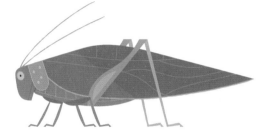

The broad-winged katydid mimics the color and texture of a leaf.

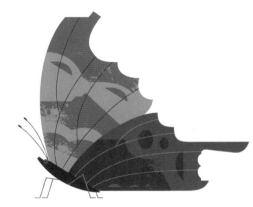

When closed, the question mark moth resembles tree bark or a dead leaf.

The caterpillar of the giant swallowtail resembles bird droppings.

ANCIENT MOUNTAINS

One of the oldest mountain ranges in the world, the Appalachians were once the height of the modern-day Rockies. Worn down over time by erosion, they're now home to strange creatures and their seasonal rituals and mysterious nocturnal displays.

FIELD SIGNALS
THE LIGHT FANTASTIC

To attract the attention of a mate, fireflies create a chemical reaction in their abdomen to light up like a lantern. Male **synchronous fireflies** of the Great Smoky Mountains will often light up all at once, creating a dazzling display.

TOOLKIT
THE OPOSSUM'S POUCH

The only marsupials native to the United States, female **Virginia opossums** have a pouch to carry their young in after they're born. After spending 70 days developing in their mother's pouch, the babies will stay close to her for several weeks, often riding on her back.

SURVIVALISTS
THE TINY TURTLE

Found mostly in meadow wetlands, the **bog turtle** is one of the rarest species of turtle in the United States. Measuring less than 4 inches long and weighing only 3 ounces, it's also the smallest.

SHELTER
MY OLD MOUNTAIN HOME

A tiny relative of the tarantula, the **spruce-fir moss spider** builds a funnel-shaped web within the moss that grows on boulders in southern Appalachian rainforests.

northern flying squirrel

northern saw-whet owl

SURVIVALISTS
AN ICE AGE FOREST

Coniferous forests (page 14) extended much farther south during the last ice age, but their range receded as the earth warmed. The climate on Southern Appalachian peaks above 5,500 feet remains cool enough to retain pockets of spruce-fir forests, preserving a home for animals now more commonly found farther north.

black-capped chickadee

red crossbill

Canada warbler

pine siskin

HUNTING
MOUNTAIN HUNTING GROUNDS

A unique group of predators dominate the Appalachian mountains: **salamanders**. Amphibians need to stay cool and moist to survive, making the rain-soaked Appalachians an ideal habitat. Almost 80 different species of salamanders can be found hunting throughout the mountains.

FIELD SIGNALS
AUTUMN BUGLE

In the fall, a mysterious song is heard in the Great Smoky Mountains. It is the bugle of the **elk**, a strange, three-octave call that bulls use to establish territory and to communicate with their herds.

Spotted salamanders live in underground burrows, emerging to hunt in the rain.

The mud salamander hunts for worms along the banks of creeks.

The long-tailed salamander hunts in forests along streams and ponds.

The giant hellbender salamander lives on the rocky bottom of mountain streams, where it feeds on crayfish, fish, and tadpoles. The largest amphibian in the United States, it can weigh up to 5 pounds and grow to over 2 feet long!

FLOWING DOWNSTREAM

The Appalachians are one of the wettest places in the eastern United States. Rain and melting snow rush downhill in swift mountain streams, eventually flowing together into larger rivers. As these rivers settle onto flat land, they began to widen and slow their pace, inviting wildlife of all kinds.

FORAGING
TOUCHY FINGERS

When **raccoons** "wash" their food before they eat, they're not cleaning up: they're learning more about their meal. Raccoons have a strong sense of touch in their fingers, and wetting their hands makes the nerves even more sensitive, helping them gather more information.

saffron shiners

TOOLKIT
FEELING FISHY

The **wavy-rayed lampmussel** relies on predatory fish to spread its larvae, so it puts out a lure that looks like a tasty smaller fish.

COMMUNITY

PUTTING OUT THE WELCOME MAT

To attract a mate, the male **river chub** uses his mouth to move up to 10,000 pebbles, building a nest that can measure 3 feet long. Other fish use his nest to lay their own eggs, which the river chub welcomes. The more eggs there are, the more likely his will remain safe from predators.

UNIFORM

SCUBA SUIT

Like all salamanders, the **hellbender salamander** breathes through its skin. Extra folds of skin along its body provide more surface area, allowing it to get more oxygen.

SHELTER
WATERFRONT DEVELOPMENT

By nesting close to water, birds can easily gather fish, worms, and aquatic insects to bring back to their chicks.

Great blue herons weave a saucer-shaped nest out of reeds, grass, and twigs.

Mallards hide their nests among reeds and grasses.

ATHLETICS
A WARM-UP STRETCH

Red-eared sliders stretch out to get as much warmth from the sun as they can while out of the water.

Belted kingfishers dig burrows in sandy riverbanks.

COMMUNITY
A QUICK GATHERING

Most **mayflies** live up to two years underwater as larvae, but only one day as adults. They take flight at the same time, gathering in huge groups to mate and lay their eggs.

TOOLKIT
THE PICKEREL'S POISON

The **pickerel frog** is the only poisonous frog in the United States: secretions in its skin make it toxic to eat.

HUNTING
STAKEOUT

The **common snapping turtle** hides along river bottoms, waiting to ambush prey as it passes by.

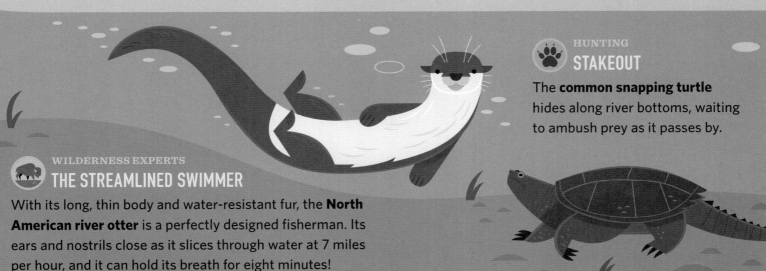

WILDERNESS EXPERTS
THE STREAMLINED SWIMMER

With its long, thin body and water-resistant fur, the **North American river otter** is a perfectly designed fisherman. Its ears and nostrils close as it slices through water at 7 miles per hour, and it can hold its breath for eight minutes!

THE FLOODING FOREST

When rivers and streams rise beyond their banks during the rainy season, floodwaters spill into neighboring hardwood forests. This can happen several times throughout the year, which periodically transforms woodlands into swamps.

SHELTER
THE FLOOD PROVIDES

A hollow log left behind by receding floodwaters makes an ideal home for a family of **bobcats**.

FIELD SIGNALS
GETTING RATTLED

With its camouflaged skin, the **timber rattlesnake** could easily be missed on the leafy forest floor, but its rattle warns off anyone who gets too close.

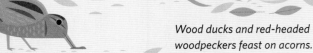

Wood ducks and red-headed woodpeckers feast on acorns.

An American woodcock feels through the soil for worms.

A nine-banded armadillo can smell grubs that are up to 8 inches underground.

FORAGING
A FOREST FEAST

In dry periods, the forest floor is rich with food. Oak trees litter the ground with acorns, and the decaying leaves and plants left by floodwater are the ideal habitat for insects, worms, and slugs.

marbled salamander

SHELTER
DEEP IN THE MUD

During dry periods, some water-loving animals bury themselves underground, waiting for the next flood.

mud turtle

digger crayfish

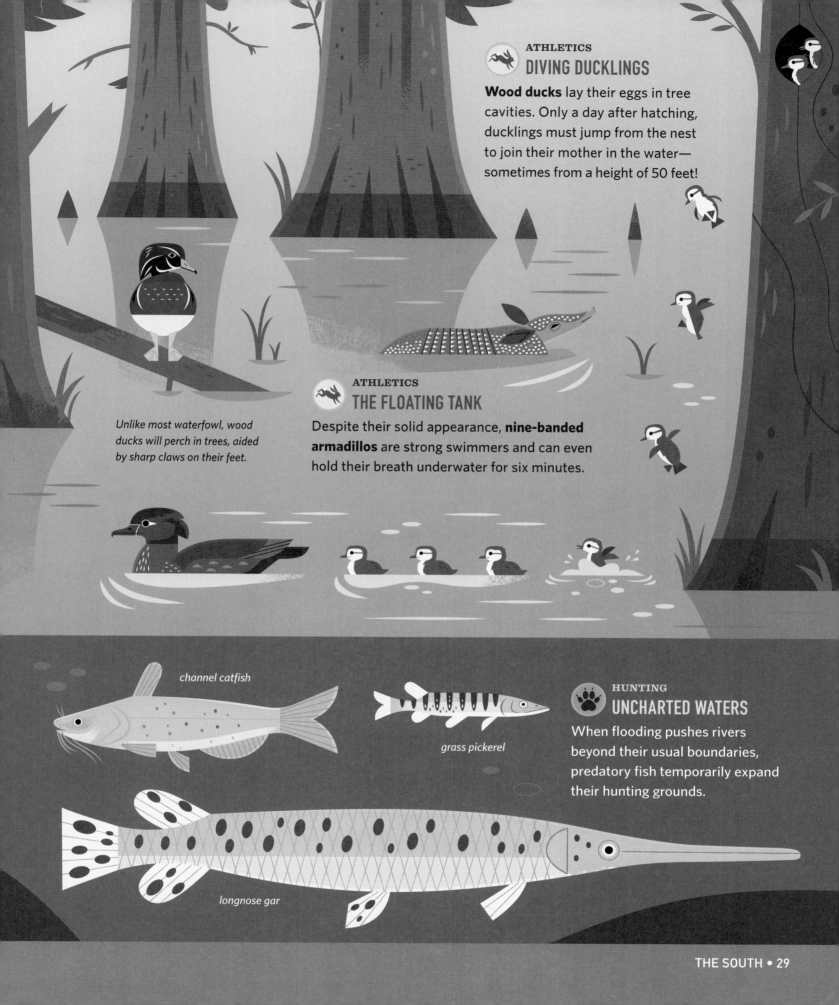

DIVING DUCKLINGS

Wood ducks lay their eggs in tree cavities. Only a day after hatching, ducklings must jump from the nest to join their mother in the water—sometimes from a height of 50 feet!

ATHLETICS
THE FLOATING TANK

Despite their solid appearance, **nine-banded armadillos** are strong swimmers and can even hold their breath underwater for six minutes.

Unlike most waterfowl, wood ducks will perch in trees, aided by sharp claws on their feet.

channel catfish

grass pickerel

HUNTING
UNCHARTED WATERS

When flooding pushes rivers beyond their usual boundaries, predatory fish temporarily expand their hunting grounds.

longnose gar

CREATURES OF THE MISSISSIPPI

Below the surface of the Mississippi River and its tributaries are some of America's most unusual creatures: giant turtles, strange amphibians, and fish species so ancient that they once swam with the dinosaurs.

 TOOLKIT
SNORKEL

The **spiny softshell turtle** uses its long, tube-like nose to breathe while underwater.

 TOOLKIT
THE CAT'S WHISKERS

The **blue catfish** has "whiskers" that are covered with taste buds, which help it locate food in muddy water.

A three-toed amphiuma can measure over 40 inches long!

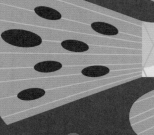

 HUNTING
TAKING RESIDENCE

The long, thin body of the **three-toed amphiuma** enables it to slip into the burrows of crayfish, its primary prey. They'll also hide out in crayfish burrows during periods of drought, emerging to hunt during rainstorms.

 NAVIGATION
A FISH OUT OF WATER

After being born in the Atlantic Ocean, **American eels** migrate upstream to live in freshwater rivers and lakes. They can survive out of water by breathing through their skin, allowing them to travel over mud and wet grass.

 TOOLKIT
A FISHING LURE

The **alligator snapping turtle** uses the worm-like appendage on the end of its tongue to draw fish into its mouth.

The largest freshwater turtle in North America, alligator snapping turtles can weigh more than 200 pounds!

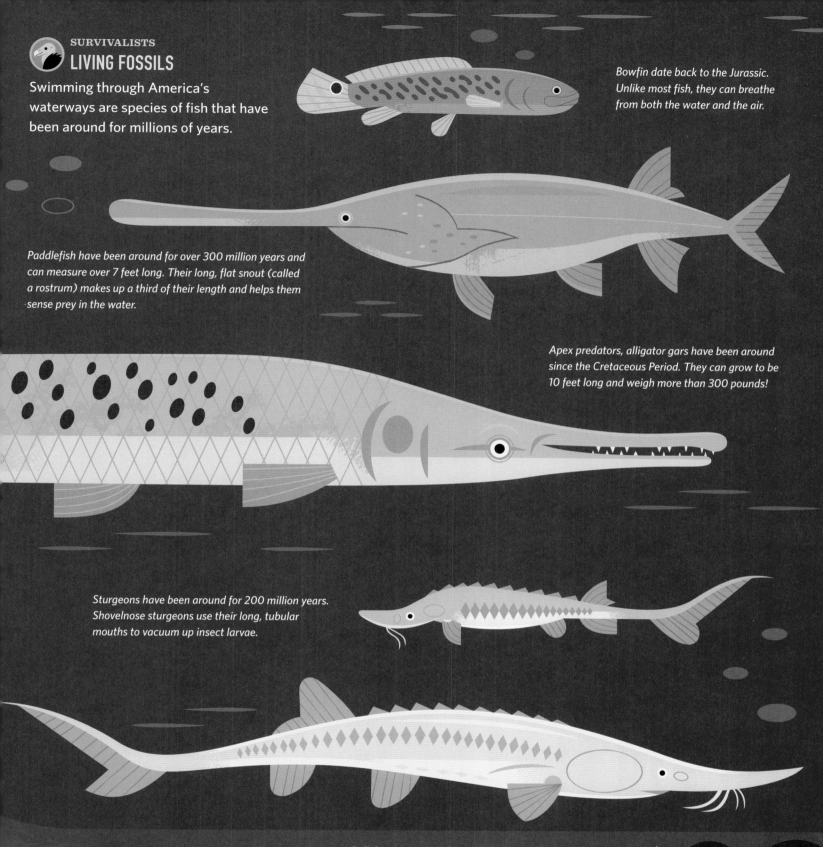

LIVING FOSSILS

Swimming through America's waterways are species of fish that have been around for millions of years.

Bowfin date back to the Jurassic. Unlike most fish, they can breathe from both the water and the air.

Paddlefish have been around for over 300 million years and can measure over 7 feet long. Their long, flat snout (called a rostrum) makes up a third of their length and helps them sense prey in the water.

Apex predators, alligator gars have been around since the Cretaceous Period. They can grow to be 10 feet long and weigh more than 300 pounds!

Sturgeons have been around for 200 million years. Shovelnose sturgeons use their long, tubular mouths to vacuum up insect larvae.

Pallid sturgeons are found in the lower Mississippi River. They also live in the shallow Missouri River of the Great Plains, where they use their fins to crawl along the muddy river bottom as they search for food.

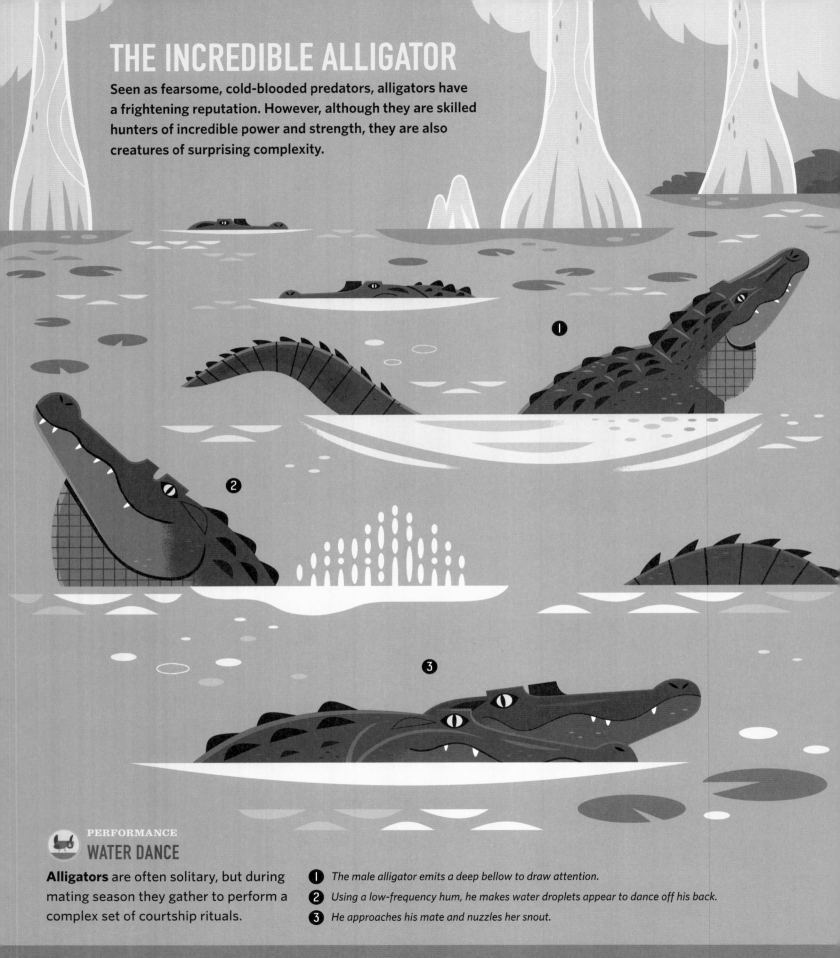

THE INCREDIBLE ALLIGATOR

Seen as fearsome, cold-blooded predators, alligators have a frightening reputation. However, although they are skilled hunters of incredible power and strength, they are also creatures of surprising complexity.

PERFORMANCE
WATER DANCE

Alligators are often solitary, but during mating season they gather to perform a complex set of courtship rituals.

1. *The male alligator emits a deep bellow to draw attention.*
2. *Using a low-frequency hum, he makes water droplets appear to dance off his back.*
3. *He approaches his mate and nuzzles her snout.*

ALLIGATORS UP ABOVE

Though they may seem heavy and sluggish, **alligators** are surprisingly good climbers. They have been found basking on tree limbs and have even been seen scaling fences!

SHELTER
THE GATOR'S NEST

Female **alligators** use their mouths to gather plants, mud, and sticks to build their nests. These mound nests, where an alligator will lay up to 60 eggs, can be 10 feet across and 3 feet tall.

Alligator mothers will stay with their young for one to two years, aggressively defending them from predators.

IDENTIFICATION
AMERICAN CROCODILIANS

The **American alligator** can be confused with the rarer **American crocodile** (page 42), but there are some key differences. Alligators prefer freshwater and live in rivers, lakes, swamps, and marshes. Crocodiles prefer saltwater and can be found along the coast. Visually, alligators are almost black in color, while crocodiles are more gray-green. To really tell them apart, we need to look at their heads.

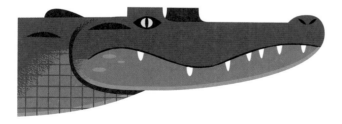

Alligators have a more rounded, U-shaped snout, and when their mouths are closed, only their upper teeth are visible.

American crocodiles have a slender, V-shaped snout, and both their upper and lower teeth are visible when their mouths are closed.

NIGHT DWELLERS

Because summers in the cypress swamp are hot and humid, many animals here wait until nightfall to become active, emerging to hunt and forage in the cooler night air.

UNIFORM
THE MASKED BANDIT

The dark fur around a **raccoon's** eyes may reduce glare, helping it see at night.

TOOLKIT
GETTING WARMER...

Water moccasins have a pit between their eyes and nostrils that can sense heat, helping them locate prey.

Known also as cottonmouths, water moccasins eat fish, frogs, and even young alligators.

HUNTING
ATTENTION GRABBING

Green herons float feathers and sticks on the water's surface to attract fish.

HUNTING
BIGMOUTH

The **American bullfrog** will eat almost anything it can capture, including fish, snakes, birds, mice, and bats!

TOOLKIT
REFLECTORS

White patches on the **bobcat's** tail and ears helps bobcat kittens follow their mother even in low light.

WILDERNESS EXPERTS
TIGER OF THE TREES

The **great horned owl** (also known as the **tiger owl**) is perfectly suited to hunt in the night. Its large eyes help it see in the dark, and its round, feathered face draws sound to its ears.

UNIFORM
CLOAK OF CONFUSION

The long tails on the **luna moth's** wings help throw off a bat's echolocation.

hoary bat

TOOLKIT
NIGHT-LIGHTS

An **alligator's** eyes reflect light, helping them see in the dark.

FORAGING
FOLLOWING HER NOSE

Virginia opossums have poor eyesight, but their strong sense of smell helps them locate food.

ATHLETICS
SWAMP SWIMMER

To escape predators, **swamp rabbits** jump into the water and paddle away.

MARSHLANDS

Along the Atlantic Ocean, water moves back and forth between sea and shore, drifting through fresh and saltwater marshes. Unlike in swamps, few trees grow in the marsh. Instead, they are filled with grasses and other soft-stemmed plants.

FRESHWATER MARSH

Rivers and streams flowing toward the ocean feed into freshwater marshes, where grasses and reeds grow in dense thickets.

NAVIGATION
SNOWBIRDS

Coastal wetlands are an important wintering ground for many different birds. **Tundra swans** migrate from their nesting sites along the Arctic ocean, some traveling almost 4,000 miles.

Muskrats use their "musky" scent to mark their territory.

Travel with the tundra swans to their nesting site on page 113.

SHELTER
UPSTAIRS NEIGHBOR

The **Canada goose** makes its nest on top of the **muskrat's** mound, taking advantage of the higher viewpoint it offers to watch for danger.

SHELTER
HOME DEVELOPER

The male **marsh wren** weaves up to 15 nests. Attracted by his singing, a female will select one and line it with leaves and grass before laying her eggs.

SURVIVALISTS
THE RED WOLF

Red wolves once roamed throughout the southern United States but were hunted to extinction in the wild. They have been reintroduced to the coastal wetlands of North Carolina, but their survival remains uncertain.

SALT MARSH

Salt marshes are found along bays and estuaries and at the mouths of rivers. The water level rises and falls twice a day with the ocean's tides.

wood storks

FORAGING
MEALTIME AT LOW TIDE

High tide brings in nutrient-rich water, feeding **oysters**, **crabs**, and **snails**. As the water retreats at low tide, these creatures are left exposed, inviting birds in search of a meal.

northern shoveler

TOOLKIT
TURTLE TEARS

To survive living in brackish water, **diamondback terrapin** have special glands that release excess salt through their tear ducts.

least tern

Wilson's plover

TOOLKIT
BOXING GLOVES

Male **fiddler crabs** have one claw that is much larger than the other, which they use to fight for territory. This claw can even be larger than their body!

SURVIVALISTS
ARRIVAL OF THE ANCIENTS

In the spring, **horseshoe crabs** arrive along the Atlantic Coast to lay their eggs in the sand. Despite their name and their aquatic lifestyle, horseshoe crabs are more related to spiders and scorpions than crustaceans. True living fossils, they've changed little over 450 million years.

NAVIGATION
STOPPING FOR A MEAL

Every year, **red knots** fly from their wintering sites in South America to nest in the Arctic, a journey of over 9,000 miles. They time their trip so that they arrive on the East Coast when the horseshoe crabs come ashore, so they can refuel by eating the crab's eggs.

UNDER THE PINES

Longleaf pines once covered the southern United States, but less than 5 percent of the original forest remains. In the surviving habitat, wildlife make their homes on the forest floor, under the sandy soils, and high in the towering pines.

UNIFORM
A DOWN-TO-EARTH STYLE

The **southeastern fox squirrel** spends lots of time on the ground, where its multicolored fur helps it camouflage among the shadowy understory.

scarlet kingsnake

coral snake

UNIFORM
A DEADLY DISGUISE

The **scarlet kingsnake** isn't venomous, but you might not know that from looking at it. Its bold red, yellow, and black stripes mimic those of the venomous **coral snake**, tricking predators into leaving it alone.

SHELTER
NO ENTRY

Southeastern pocket gophers plug the entrances to their burrows to keep snakes from entering.

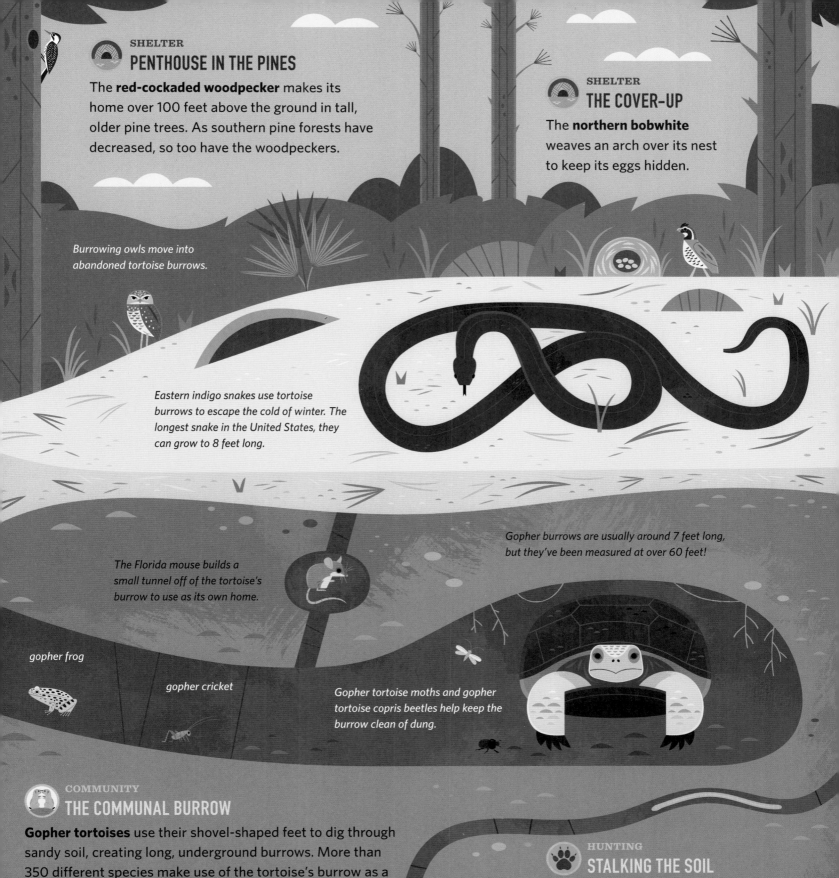

PENTHOUSE IN THE PINES

The **red-cockaded woodpecker** makes its home over 100 feet above the ground in tall, older pine trees. As southern pine forests have decreased, so too have the woodpeckers.

THE COVER-UP

The **northern bobwhite** weaves an arch over its nest to keep its eggs hidden.

Burrowing owls move into abandoned tortoise burrows.

Eastern indigo snakes use tortoise burrows to escape the cold of winter. The longest snake in the United States, they can grow to 8 feet long.

Gopher burrows are usually around 7 feet long, but they've been measured at over 60 feet!

The Florida mouse builds a small tunnel off of the tortoise's burrow to use as its own home.

gopher frog

gopher cricket

Gopher tortoise moths and gopher tortoise copris beetles help keep the burrow clean of dung.

THE COMMUNAL BURROW

Gopher tortoises use their shovel-shaped feet to dig through sandy soil, creating long, underground burrows. More than 350 different species make use of the tortoise's burrow as a home, a seasonal den for hibernation, or a temporary escape from bad weather or forest fires.

STALKING THE SOIL

Florida worm lizards hunt through the sand for spiders, worms, and termites.

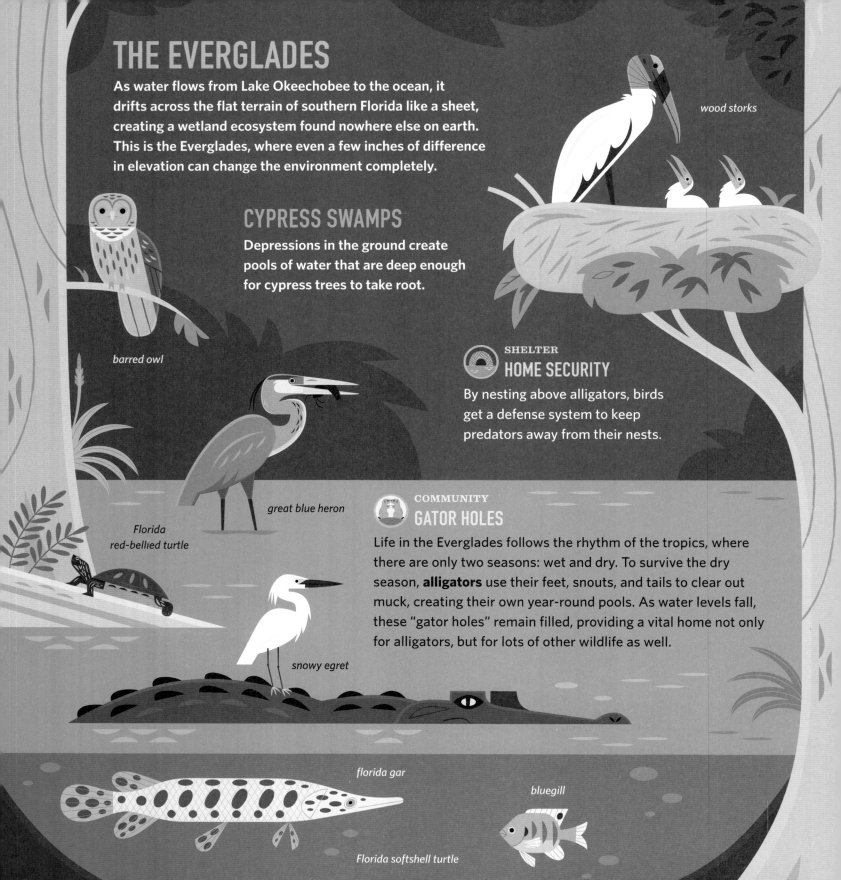

THE EVERGLADES

As water flows from Lake Okeechobee to the ocean, it drifts across the flat terrain of southern Florida like a sheet, creating a wetland ecosystem found nowhere else on earth. This is the Everglades, where even a few inches of difference in elevation can change the environment completely.

wood storks

CYPRESS SWAMPS

Depressions in the ground create pools of water that are deep enough for cypress trees to take root.

barred owl

SHELTER
HOME SECURITY

By nesting above alligators, birds get a defense system to keep predators away from their nests.

great blue heron

Florida red-bellied turtle

COMMUNITY
GATOR HOLES

Life in the Everglades follows the rhythm of the tropics, where there are only two seasons: wet and dry. To survive the dry season, **alligators** use their feet, snouts, and tails to clear out muck, creating their own year-round pools. As water levels fall, these "gator holes" remain filled, providing a vital home not only for alligators, but for lots of other wildlife as well.

snowy egret

florida gar

bluegill

Florida softshell turtle

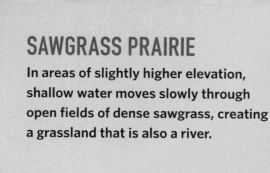

SAWGRASS PRAIRIE

In areas of slightly higher elevation, shallow water moves slowly through open fields of dense sawgrass, creating a grassland that is also a river.

HARDWOOD HAMMOCKS

Forests of tropical hardwood trees grow on islands that rise above the water level.

ATHLETICS
AERIAL ACROBAT

Swallow-tailed kites roll, dive backward, and swiftly turn midair to catch flying insects.

great egret

SURVIVALISTS
PANTHER OF THE EVERGLADES

The dry land of the hardwood hammocks offers refuge to **Florida panthers**, the last remaining mountain lions in the eastern United States.

FORAGING
THE WET GRASSLAND

White-tailed deer feed on sawgrass, while wading birds search the marsh for fish, insects, and crustaceans.

little blue heron

TOOLKIT
GET THE HOOK

In the Everglades, the **snail kite** feeds almost entirely on **Florida apple snails**, using its hooked beak to pull them from their shells.

TROPICAL AMERICA

Southern Florida's subtropical climate stays warm all year, making it a haven for creatures more commonly found in Central and South America.

UNIFORM
WARDROBE CHANGE

During the breeding season, some of the most beautiful birds in the Everglades become even more striking as they change their plumage to attract a mate.

COMMUNITY
INFORMATION CENTER

Black vultures roost in groups, exchanging information about where they have found food.

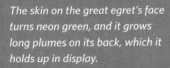

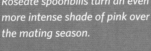

The skin on the great egret's face turns neon green, and it grows long plumes on its back, which it holds up in display.

Roseate spoonbills turn an even more intense shade of pink over the mating season.

SURVIVALISTS
RETURN OF THE CROCODILE

The **American crocodile's** home ranges from Peru to Mexico, but within the United States it lives only in southern Florida. By the 1970s habitat loss and hunting had reduced their local population to only a few hundred, but with federal protection, their numbers have begun to increase.

Southern Florida is the only place in the world where alligators and crocodiles share the same habitat.

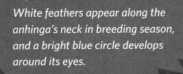

White feathers appear along the anhinga's neck in breeding season, and a bright blue circle develops around its eyes.

TOOLKIT
WADING BOOTS

The long toes of the **purple gallinule** allow it to walk over water, stepping on grasses and floating plants as it feeds.

Algae often grows on the backs of slow-moving manatees, providing a feast for bluegills and other fish.

Manatees may look more like a walrus or seal, but their closest relatives are actually elephants.

NAVIGATION

WHERE THE SEA COWS ROAM

Despite their bulky appearance, **Florida manatees** have very little body fat, so they can't survive in cold water. They spend the winter upriver, where Florida's natural springs help keep them warm. In the spring, they return to coastal waters, where they'll graze on beds of seagrass. Though they generally stay around Florida, they've been recorded as far west as Texas and as far north as Rhode Island!

THE FOREST IN THE SEA

The shorelines of southern Florida and the Caribbean are fringed with forests of mangroves. Short trees with dense tangles of roots, mangroves are adapted to survive in places where fresh and salty water meet.

HUNTING
THE FEATHERED FISHERMAN

With water-resistant feathers and long, hook-like talons, **osprey** are perfectly designed to catch fish, which make up 99 percent of their diet.

roseate spoonbills

FORAGING
THE TREE CRAB

The **mangrove tree crab** feeds on leaves at high tide, moving to the tree's roots to scavenge for bits of plant and animal material at low tide.

HUNTING
LYING IN WAIT

The **American crocodile** floats perfectly still in the water, waiting to capture unsuspecting prey.

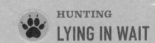

TOOLKIT
A SENSITIVE SAW

The **smalltooth sawfish** uses its rostrum, a long and sensitive snout that is shaped like a saw, to feel for crabs and fish in the sand and mud.

TOOLKIT
THE HORSE'S LASSO

A poor swimmer, the **longsnout seahorse** uses its prehensile tail to hold on to mangrove roots, waiting to grab zooplankton as it drifts past.

FORAGING
THE UPSIDE-DOWN JELLYFISH

Cassiopea jellyfish lie upside down so the algae living within their tissue can use sunlight for photosynthesis, creating food that feeds the jellyfish.

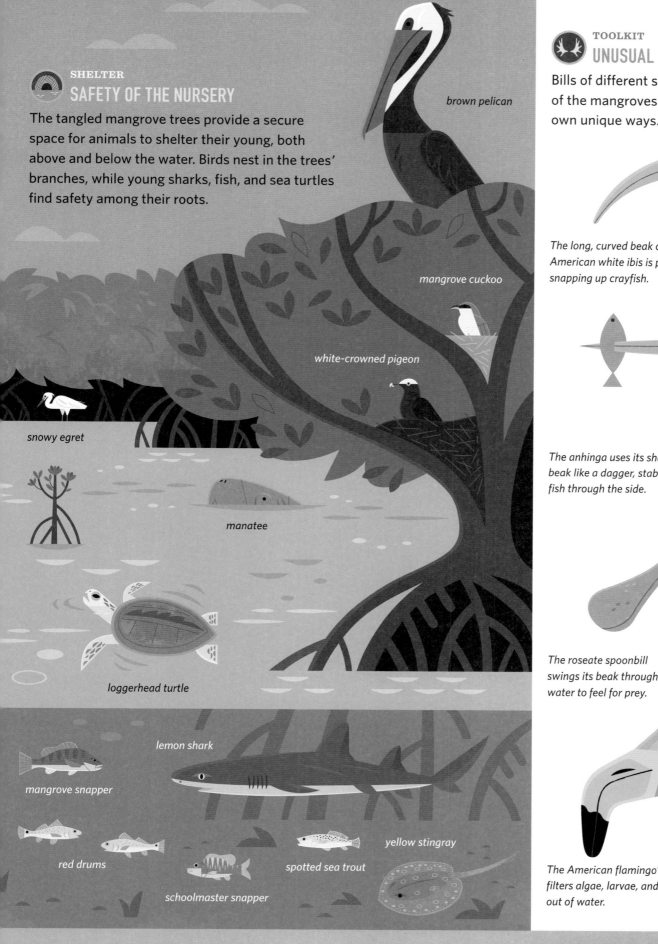

SHELTER
SAFETY OF THE NURSERY

The tangled mangrove trees provide a secure space for animals to shelter their young, both above and below the water. Birds nest in the trees' branches, while young sharks, fish, and sea turtles find safety among their roots.

brown pelican

mangrove cuckoo

white-crowned pigeon

snowy egret

manatee

loggerhead turtle

lemon shark

mangrove snapper

red drums

schoolmaster snapper

spotted sea trout

yellow stingray

UNUSUAL BILLS

Bills of different shapes allow the birds of the mangroves to each feed in their own unique ways.

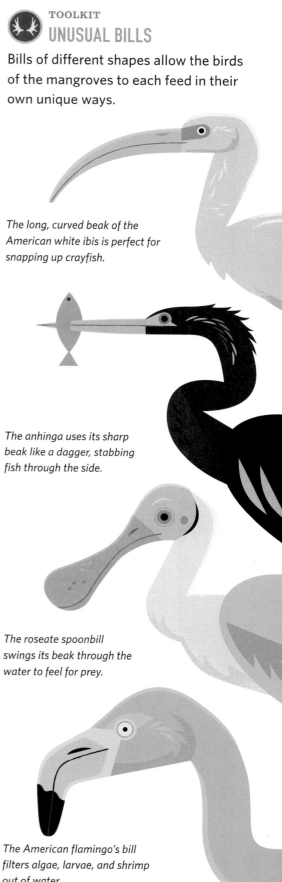

The long, curved beak of the American white ibis is perfect for snapping up crayfish.

The anhinga uses its sharp beak like a dagger, stabbing fish through the side.

The roseate spoonbill swings its beak through the water to feel for prey.

The American flamingo's bill filters algae, larvae, and shrimp out of water.

ISLANDS OF THE CARIBBEAN

On the eastern edge of the Caribbean Sea, the territories of Puerto Rico and the United States Virgin Islands offer habitat both on land and in the surrounding sea.

HUNTING
THE FISHING BAT

The **greater bulldog bat** finds fish by using echolocation to sense ripples they make in the water, then snatches them with its clawed feet.

FORAGING
UNDERWATER GRASSLANDS

Beneath the waves offshore, fields of seagrass provide foraging grounds for animals of all sizes.

HUNTING
BUGGED OUT

Puerto Rican todies consume about 40 percent of their body weight in insects every day.

HUNTING
HANGING AROUND

Puerto Rican boas hang outside of caves at dusk, waiting to capture bats as they emerge.

Antillean fruit bats

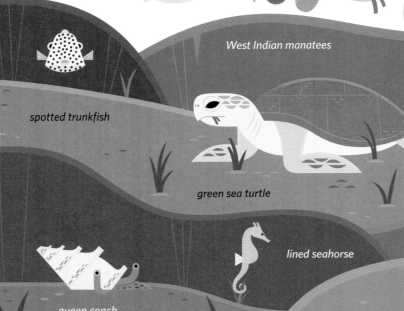

West Indian manatees

The largest aquatic herbivores in the world, manatees can weigh over 1,000 pounds and eat up to 100 pounds of plants a day.

spotted trunkfish

green sea turtle

lined seahorse

queen conch

Southern stingrays swim low over the seagrass, searching for fish and crabs.

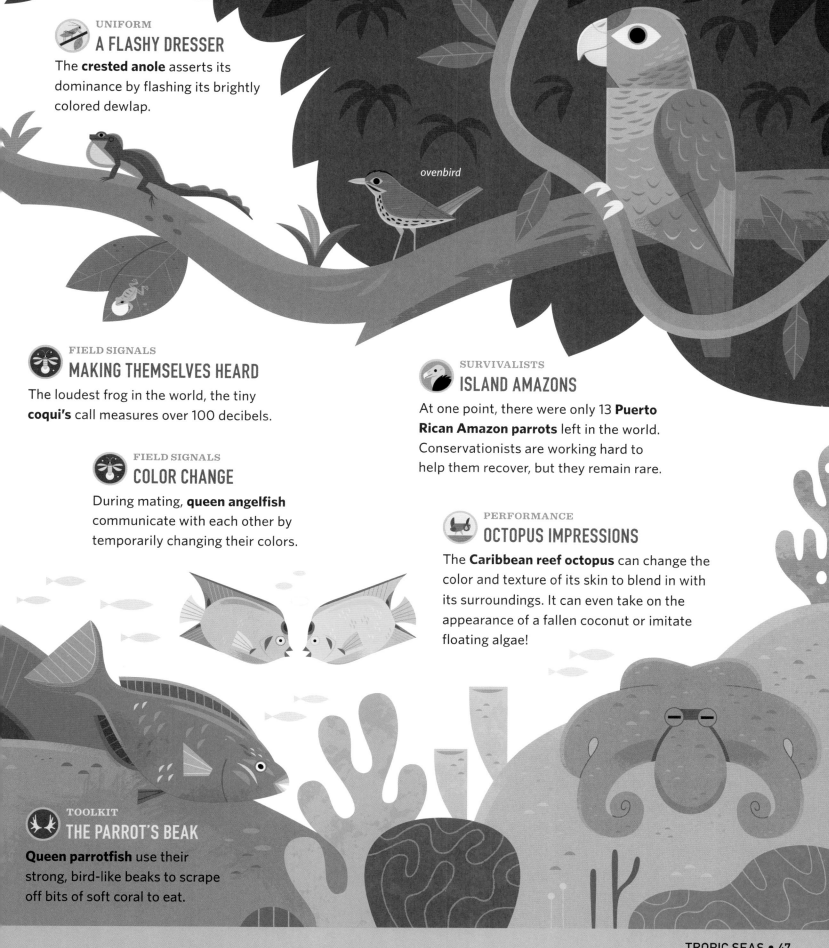

UNIFORM
A FLASHY DRESSER

The **crested anole** asserts its dominance by flashing its brightly colored dewlap.

ovenbird

FIELD SIGNALS
MAKING THEMSELVES HEARD

The loudest frog in the world, the tiny **coqui's** call measures over 100 decibels.

FIELD SIGNALS
COLOR CHANGE

During mating, **queen angelfish** communicate with each other by temporarily changing their colors.

SURVIVALISTS
ISLAND AMAZONS

At one point, there were only 13 **Puerto Rican Amazon parrots** left in the world. Conservationists are working hard to help them recover, but they remain rare.

PERFORMANCE
OCTOPUS IMPRESSIONS

The **Caribbean reef octopus** can change the color and texture of its skin to blend in with its surroundings. It can even take on the appearance of a fallen coconut or imitate floating algae!

TOOLKIT
THE PARROT'S BEAK

Queen parrotfish use their strong, bird-like beaks to scrape off bits of soft coral to eat.

THE SEA MEETS THE PRAIRIE

Worlds converge in southern Texas, a place where coastal grasslands meet mesquite shrubland on the shores of the Gulf of Mexico. Migrating animals arrive by sea and air, mixing with wildlife from both Mexico and the United States.

COMMUNITY
STORMING THE BEACH

Female **Kemp's ridley sea turtles** arrive ashore in groups called arribadas (Spanish for "arrivals"), laying their eggs in the sand at the same time. By all coming ashore together to lay so many eggs at once, they may reduce the chance that their own eggs will be the ones eaten by predators.

A black vulture (left) and a crested caracara (above) wait to dig up sea turtle eggs.

TOOLKIT
THE LITTLE ARMORED ONE

Bony, armor-like plates cover the bodies of **nine-banded armadillos**, protecting them from predators.

green jay

UNIFORM
THE OCELOT'S SPOTS

The **ocelot's** spotted coat helps it camouflage as it moves through the shadowy brush in search of prey.

Travel west into the desert to page 72 to see which other animals live in the borderlands.

NAVIGATION

WALTZ ACROSS TEXAS

With its temperate climate, Texas is able to serve as a crossroads for migratory species throughout the year. Its coastal marshlands are a wintering spot for wildlife from the north and a summer breeding site for animals from the south. Further west, animals pass through Texas along migration corridors that take them to Mexico and beyond.

Wilson's plovers arrive in the spring, nesting on beaches and salt flats where they'll be close to their preferred prey of fiddler crabs.

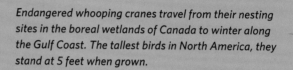

Endangered whooping cranes travel from their nesting sites in the boreal wetlands of Canada to winter along the Gulf Coast. The tallest birds in North America, they stand at 5 feet when grown.

Roseate spoonbills arrive from Mexico and Central America in the summer.

green darner

Though some black-bellied whistling ducks live in southern Texas year-round, many migrate to Mexico for the winter.

Rufous hummingbirds cross west Texas in the fall on their way to Mexico. Follow the hummingbird to page 81.

Alligators live in the marshlands of the Gulf Coast, ranging as far west as the Rio Grande.

Monarch butterflies travel through Texas on their way to Mexico in the fall, and again in the spring as they return north.

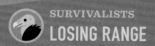

SURVIVALISTS

LOSING RANGE

Attwater's prairie chickens once lived in large numbers throughout the coastal grasslands of Louisiana and Texas, but loss of habitat and changes to their ecosystem have pushed them to the edge of extinction.

SHELTER

UNDER THE PRICKLY PEAR

Unlike its larger relatives in the south (page 39) and the west (page 80), the **Texas tortoise** doesn't dig a burrow. Instead, it uses its claws to scrape out a resting place under a cactus or a bush.

THE AERIAL HIGHWAY

Seasonal wildlife migrations were once a part of life in the Great Plains. As wild spaces disappeared and fences went up, many of these ancient routes were cut off, but one route remains open: the sky.

Snow geese often travel in flocks of over 1,000 birds.

turkey vulture

golden plover

northern pintail

black-chinned hummingbird

canvasback

scissor-tailed flycatcher

Bonaparte's gull

upland sandpiper

black tern

The bobolink migrates to and from South America, a round-trip journey of 12,000 miles.

ferruginous hawk

yellow-billed cuckoo

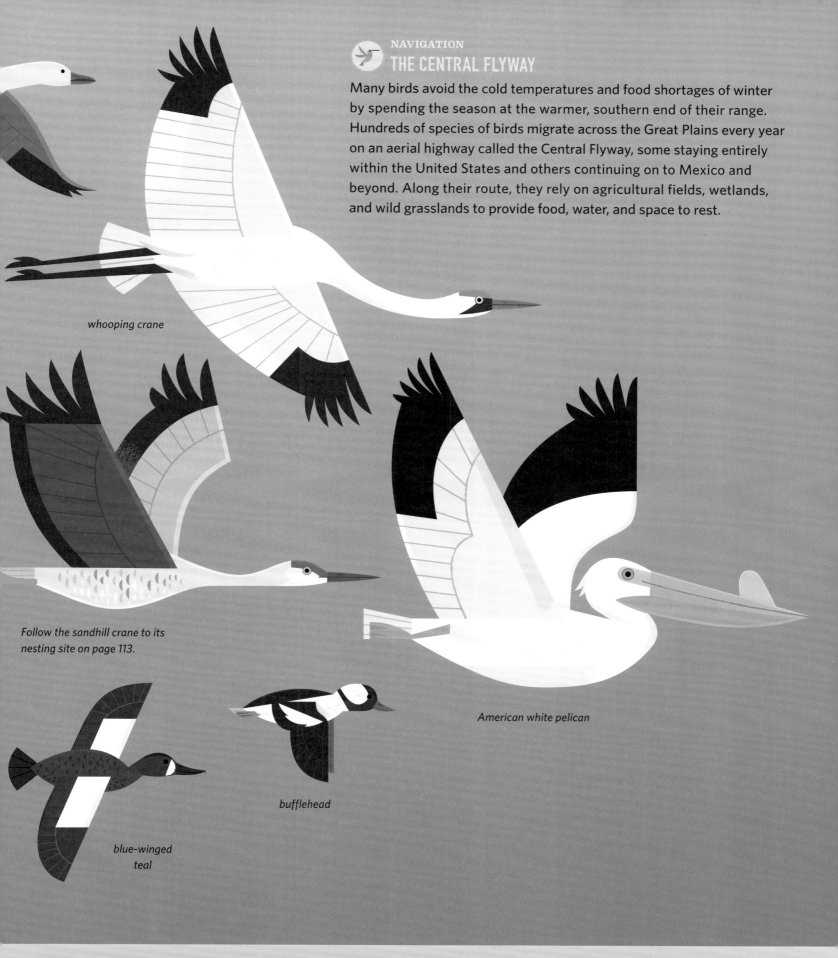

Many birds avoid the cold temperatures and food shortages of winter by spending the season at the warmer, southern end of their range. Hundreds of species of birds migrate across the Great Plains every year on an aerial highway called the Central Flyway, some staying entirely within the United States and others continuing on to Mexico and beyond. Along their route, they rely on agricultural fields, wetlands, and wild grasslands to provide food, water, and space to rest.

whooping crane

Follow the sandhill crane to its nesting site on page 113.

American white pelican

bufflehead

blue-winged teal

LAND OF THE BISON

The interior of the United States was at one time a vast grassland, the domain of the largest animal in the Americas: the bison. Herds of bison once roamed the Great Plains in the millions, playing a vital role in the ecology of the grasslands and supporting other wildlife in surprising ways.

In the winter, pronghorns rely on bison to help clear snow to get to the plants underneath.

By keeping grasses short, bison give prairie dogs a clearer view of potential danger from their guard posts.

WILDERNESS EXPERTS

GIANTS OF THE GRASSLAND

The seasons vary widely in America's temperate grasslands, but **bison** are adapted to face the challenges they present. They graze through the winter by using their large shoulder humps to swing their heads through snow, clearing it to get to the grass underneath. In the summer, they shed their thick wool coats and take frequent dirt baths to clean themselves of flies. If summer insects are particularly bothersome, they rub their horns on trees to release strong-smelling sap, creating a natural repellant.

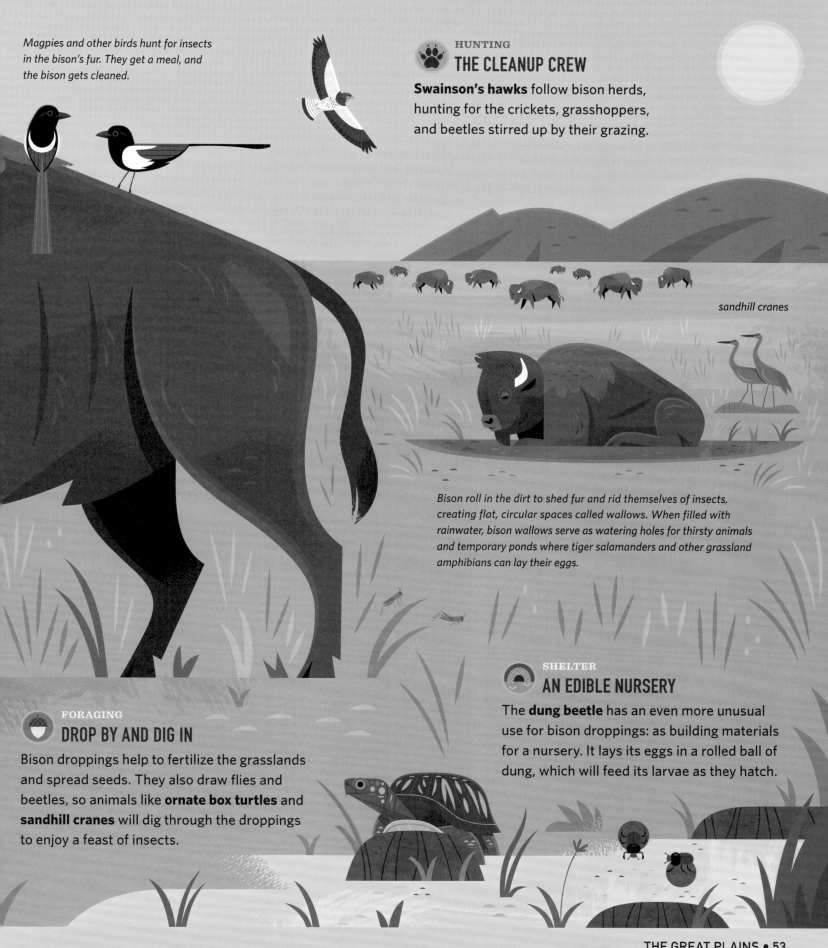

Magpies and other birds hunt for insects in the bison's fur. They get a meal, and the bison gets cleaned.

THE CLEANUP CREW

Swainson's hawks follow bison herds, hunting for the crickets, grasshoppers, and beetles stirred up by their grazing.

sandhill cranes

Bison roll in the dirt to shed fur and rid themselves of insects, creating flat, circular spaces called wallows. When filled with rainwater, bison wallows serve as watering holes for thirsty animals and temporary ponds where tiger salamanders and other grassland amphibians can lay their eggs.

SHELTER
AN EDIBLE NURSERY

The **dung beetle** has an even more unusual use for bison droppings: as building materials for a nursery. It lays its eggs in a rolled ball of dung, which will feed its larvae as they hatch.

FORAGING
DROP BY AND DIG IN

Bison droppings help to fertilize the grasslands and spread seeds. They also draw flies and beetles, so animals like **ornate box turtles** and **sandhill cranes** will dig through the droppings to enjoy a feast of insects.

COURTSHIP ON THE PRAIRIE

Throughout the spring and summer, animals all across the Great Plains compete for the attention of a mate. They fight for territory, display their best physical features, and engage in elaborate courtship rituals.

 FIELD SIGNALS
A MESSAGE IN THE DUST

During rutting season, the **bison** bull rolls in the dirt, creating enormous clouds of dust that advertise his strength and power to both potential mates and rivals. If he is challenged by another bull, they'll face off in head-to-head combat.

 **ATHLETICS**
LOCKING HORNS

To protect their territory, male **pronghorns** lock horns with their rivals, trying to overpower them.

ATHLETICS
RATTLER WRESTLING

During the mating season, male **prairie rattlesnakes** engage in a "combat dance" to establish dominance.

 PERFORMANCE
CHICKEN DANCE

Male **greater prairie chickens** take to open spaces called leks to perform some of the most elaborate courtship displays in the grasslands. They extend their necks, lower their wings, then stamp their feet and click their feathers while using the air sacs on their necks to make a booming sound.

 PERFORMANCE
WATER BALLET

Migrating birds turn the prairie's wetlands into a stage, performing a range of dramatic courtship displays.

When selecting their mate, sandhill cranes join in a dance, bowing to each other, then leaping into the air with their wings outstretched.

White pelicans nod their heads to prospective mates, showing off their bright orange bills.

Before singing, the red-winged blackbird hunches forward to show off his bold red epaulets.

After mating, American avocets cross their bills and march together.

During courtship, the hooded merganser sings a low, frog-like song.

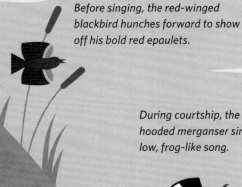

Pairs of western grebes bond through a dance in which they run together across the water's surface.

The male redhead performs a head throw to attract attention, pulling its head back and remaining perfectly still on the water.

Male ruddy ducks attract females by beating their bright blue bills against their chest to create bubbles.

AMERICAN GRASSLANDS

The Great Plains were at one time a mosaic of different grassland ecosystems. Lush tallgrass prairie grew in the east, the dry shortgrass prairie stretched across the west, and they met in the middle in the mixed-grass prairie. Today, only fragments of these environments remain.

TALLGRASS PRAIRIE

In the eastern Great Plains, heavy summer rainfall helps grasses grow up to 10 feet tall. With environmental conditions well suited for agriculture, most tallgrass prairie has been lost to farmland and development.

FORAGING
GRASSES FOR GRAZING

Over 70 species of grass grow in the tallgrass prairie. Fast growing and plentiful, grass is an important food source for a variety of animals, both large and small.

eastern cottontail

grasshopper sparrow

FORAGING
PICKY EATERS

Monarch butterflies rely on the presence of milkweed along their migration routes. They lay their eggs on milkweed leaves because it is the only plant their caterpillars will eat.

Migrate with the monarch butterflies to page 49.

SHELTER
AMONG THE GRASS

To keep their nests safe, **western meadowlarks** build their nests deep within tall grass, sometimes beyond an entrance tunnel that's several feet long.

UNIFORM
VERTICAL STRIPES

The **thirteen-lined ground squirrel's** patterned coat helps it to camouflage among the blades of grass.

SHORTGRASS PRAIRIE

The western Great Plains sit in the rain shadow of the Rocky Mountains, creating an arid landscape where plants rarely grow higher than a foot tall.

FORAGING
PICKING UP THE SCENT

Turkey vultures have a strong sense of smell, which helps them detect carrion from long distances.

ATHLETICS
TRACK STARS

The open spaces of the shortgrass prairie leave few places to hide, making speed a key tool of survival.

Bison, swift foxes, and black-tailed jackrabbits can all run at 40 miles per hour.

Able to run over 60 miles per hour, pronghorns are the fastest land animals in the Americas.

HUNTING
FLYING LOW

The **northern harrier** flies low over the ground, the stiff feathers around its face directing the sound of mice and voles to its ears.

prairie rattlesnake

greater short-horned lizard

UNIFORM
COLOR CLASH

To survive out in the open, the **rainbow grasshopper** takes the opposite approach. Its pattern of bold hues warns predators that it has a foul taste.

UNIFORM
THE PRAIRIE LOOK

Exposed on the open grassland, some reptiles use mottled camouflage to blend in with the dirt and dry grass.

IN THE DIRT

Without the cover of tall grass, many animals in the mixed and shortgrass prairies choose to go underground to find shelter. Few animals on the Great Plains do this as successfully as the prairie dog, whose tunneling lifestyle supports the grassland ecosystem in countless ways.

Sentinels stand guard while other prairie dogs graze, and give a warning with a high-pitched alarm call. They have unique calls to identify different predators.

By eating the grasses that grow around their burrows, prairie dogs clear room for the higher-nutrition weeds and plants that bison and other grazers like to eat.

Prairie dogs "kiss" to identify other members of their family group.

HUNTING
A TIGHT FIT

The **American badger** digs into the ground to pursue prey, its flat body helping it squeeze through underground tunnels.

Black-tailed prairie dogs take turns stretching tall and barking in a "jump-yip" to check in with one another.

COMMUNITY
UNDERGROUND SOCIETY

Black-tailed prairie dogs dig burrows to serve as a shelter from predators and a retreat from the extreme weather of the Great Plains. Multiple family groups build their burrows close together, forming prairie dog "towns." Living close together allows prairie dogs to watch out for one another, but their towns are also vital to the health of the grassland ecosystem in many ways. Their tunneling aerates the soil, their abandoned burrows make an ideal home for other animals, and they're a vital food source for many grassland predators.

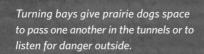

Turning bays give prairie dogs space to pass one another in the tunnels or to listen for danger outside.

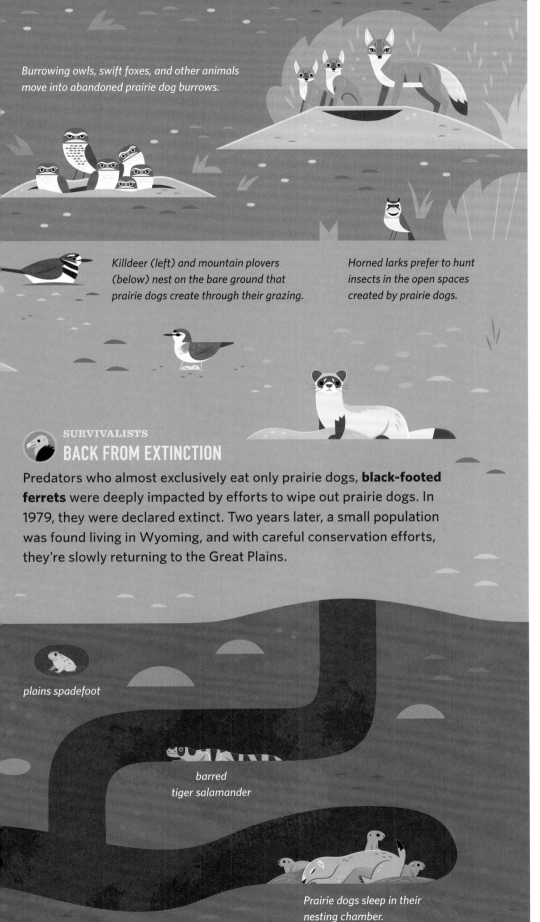

Burrowing owls, swift foxes, and other animals move into abandoned prairie dog burrows.

Killdeer (left) and mountain plovers (below) nest on the bare ground that prairie dogs create through their grazing.

Horned larks prefer to hunt insects in the open spaces created by prairie dogs.

BACK FROM EXTINCTION

Predators who almost exclusively eat only prairie dogs, **black-footed ferrets** were deeply impacted by efforts to wipe out prairie dogs. In 1979, they were declared extinct. Two years later, a small population was found living in Wyoming, and with careful conservation efforts, they're slowly returning to the Great Plains.

plains spadefoot

barred tiger salamander

Prairie dogs sleep in their nesting chamber.

EXCAVATORS

The animals of the plains are equipped with some very different tools to help them get underground.

Strong claws help prairie dogs tunnel through soil.

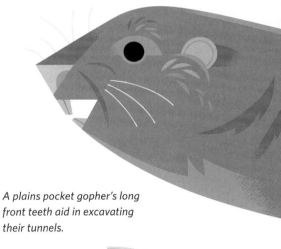

A plains pocket gopher's long front teeth aid in excavating their tunnels.

Hard growths on the spadefoot's hind feet help it dig.

The western hognose snake uses its upturned snout to move through sand and dirt.

GRIZZLY COUNTRY

North American brown bears, known also as grizzlies, once roamed throughout the mixed and shortgrass prairies. As the United States expanded its territory in the 1800s, settlers drove them from the plains, and for decades, the surviving grizzlies found refuge in the Rocky Mountains. In recent years, some bears have begun venturing back onto the grasslands of Montana, suggesting a possible future for grizzlies on the Great Plains.

SHELTER

HOME EXCAVATION

Grizzlies dig their winter dens into steep mountain slopes, where heavy snowfall will help to insulate them throughout the winter. When building a den, a grizzly might dig out 2,000 pounds of material!

FIELD SIGNALS

THE MESSAGE TREE

After emerging from hibernartion, **grizzlies** scratch their backs against trees, leaving behind bits of fur. This helps shed their winter fur, but it also marks the tree with their unique scent, letting other bears know that they're in the area.

TOOLKIT

BETTER THAN A BLOODHOUND

After months of not eating, **grizzlies** wake up particularly hungry. Their strong sense of smell helps them sniff out the carcasses of animals revealed by the melting snow.

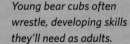

Young bear cubs often wrestle, developing skills they'll need as adults.

FORAGING
THE LITTLE THINGS

To build up enough fat to survive their winter hibernation, **grizzlies** spend the summer and autumn eating as much as they can. And though a grizzly will hunt on occasion, large prey animals are not central to their diet. For grizzlies to get big, they have to think small.

Miller moths escape the heat of summer in the Great Plains by migrating to the slopes of the Rocky Mountains. Grizzlies lift rocks to get to the fat-rich moths underneath, eating up to 40,000 in a single day!

The grizzly's claws come in handy for tearing open tree stumps for grubs or for digging into the earth to feast on ants.

Over 60 percent of the grizzly's diet is made up of plant matter like berries, grasses, and roots.

IDENTIFICATION
BEARS OF THE ROCKIES

Both **grizzlies** and **black bears** live in the Northern Rocky Mountains: grizzlies in the alpine tundra and on open plains, black bears in mountain forests. Visually, both species of bear can have fur that ranges from black to cinnamon in color, making them difficult to tell apart, so we use these tools instead.

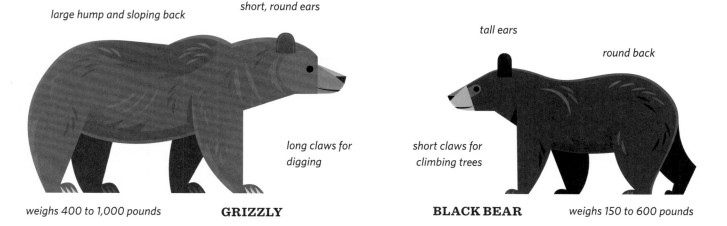

large hump and sloping back

short, round ears

tall ears

round back

long claws for digging

short claws for climbing trees

weighs 400 to 1,000 pounds   **GRIZZLY**

BLACK BEAR   *weighs 150 to 600 pounds*

WINTER IN YELLOWSTONE

Spread across a giant supervolcano in the Rocky Mountains, most of Yellowstone rises over 6,000 feet in elevation. Winters here are among the coldest in the lower United States, with subzero temperatures and months of snow.

FORAGING
THAWING DINNER

With most of Yellowstone's vegetation buried under deep snow, **bison** make use of the area's geothermal sites, where the heat from springs and geysers keep snow levels lower.

ATHLETICS
WINTER SPORTS

River otters play together in the snow, sledding down riverbanks and hillsides. This activity helps them bond and strengthen their hunting skills.

HUNTING
DEEP LISTENING

The **great gray owl's** powerful hearing helps it detect prey moving over a foot beneath the snow. To catch it, the owl dives down talons-first into the snow.

NAVIGATION
FAMILY REUNION

Only a few dozen **trumpeter swans** live in Yellowstone year-round, but in the winter they're joined by thousands more from across Canada and the Rocky Mountains.

The largest waterfowl in North America, trumpeter swans have a wingspan of up to 8 feet.

COMMUNITY
FOLLOW THE LEADER

Moving through deep snow is strenuous work. To conserve energy, **elk** herds walk in single file, the leader helping to clear the snow for the others.

Coyotes and mapgpies hang back, waiting to fight ravens for the scraps.

COMMUNITY
A NEIGHBORHOOD HOT SPOT

An animal that has died in the snow becomes a meeting point for Yellowstone's predators and scavengers. **Ravens** lead **gray wolves** to dead animals, because wolves can open a carcass more easily than they can.

THE RUGGED MOUNTAINSIDE

Made up of over 100 separate mountain ranges, the Rocky Mountains stretch 3,000 miles from Canada to New Mexico. The highest peaks in the Rocky Mountains tower over 14,000 feet above sea level, and their sheer cliffs and rushing rivers present a challenging terrain for wildlife.

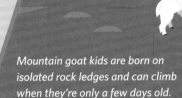

NAVIGATION
A VERTICAL MIGRATION

Mountain goats spend the winter at lower elevations, eating from pines and shrubs. In the summer they climb to the high tundra, where they enjoy the cool air and feed on lichen and moss.

Mountain goat kids are born on isolated rock ledges and can climb when they're only a few days old.

UNIFORM
LIFE VEST

Harlequin ducks dive into the rapids to find food. Air trapped in their feathers helps them bounce back to the surface.

HUNTING
FISH-EYED

Cutthroat trout use their keen vision to hunt mountain streams for insects, worms, and small amphibians.

SURVIVALISTS
MAKING IT BACK HOME

Sockeye salmon used to migrate from the Pacific Ocean to the Sawtooth Mountains of Idaho in large numbers, but dams built along their route made the already difficult journey nearly impossible. Conservation efforts are now underway to help their population recover.

To reach the Sawtooth Mountains, sockeye salmon travel over 900 miles and climb an elevation of more than 6,000 feet. *Travel to page 100 to see where their journey begins.*

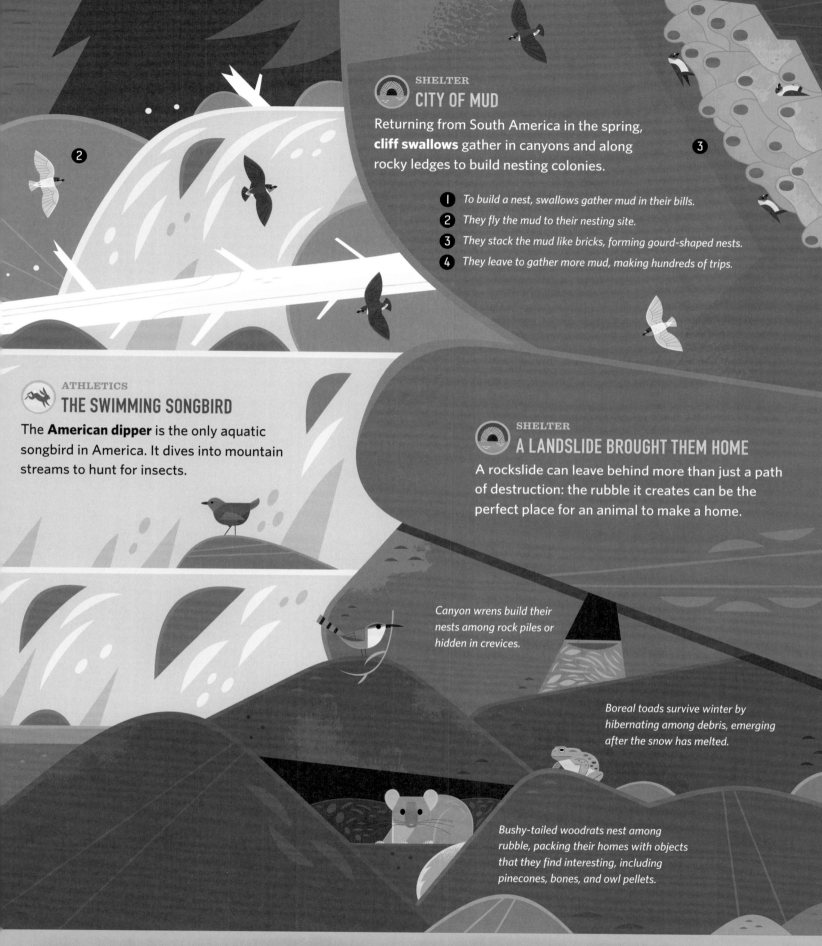

SHELTER
CITY OF MUD

Returning from South America in the spring, **cliff swallows** gather in canyons and along rocky ledges to build nesting colonies.

1 *To build a nest, swallows gather mud in their bills.*
2 *They fly the mud to their nesting site.*
3 *They stack the mud like bricks, forming gourd-shaped nests.*
4 *They leave to gather more mud, making hundreds of trips.*

ATHLETICS
THE SWIMMING SONGBIRD

The **American dipper** is the only aquatic songbird in America. It dives into mountain streams to hunt for insects.

SHELTER
A LANDSLIDE BROUGHT THEM HOME

A rockslide can leave behind more than just a path of destruction: the rubble it creates can be the perfect place for an animal to make a home.

Canyon wrens build their nests among rock piles or hidden in crevices.

Boreal toads survive winter by hibernating among debris, emerging after the snow has melted.

Bushy-tailed woodrats nest among rubble, packing their homes with objects that they find interesting, including pinecones, bones, and owl pellets.

ON TOP OF THE WORLD

High in the Rockies lies the alpine tundra, a windswept and treeless environment. Winters here are brutal, and many mountain residents either migrate elsewhere or spend the season hibernating. In the summer, wildflowers bloom, and the environment is alive with high-altitude life.

COMMUNITY
SUMMER OF THE MARMOTS

Yellow-bellied marmots spend up to eight months hibernating in underground burrows, in colonies of 10 to 20 individuals. They emerge in the spring, ready for a very busy season on the alpine tundra.

One marmot stands guard, giving a sharp whistle to warn the others of danger.

While out of the burrow, marmots bask in the sun for warmth.

HUNTING
THE MIGHTY GOLDEN EAGLE

With a 7-foot wingspan and 3-inch-long talons, a **golden eagle** is large and powerful enough to take down a young mountain goat.

Marmots spend summer preparing for their winter hibernation by fattening up on grasses, flowers, and insects.

Young marmots will often engage in play-fighting.

SHELTER
A REMOTE CHALET

Gray-crowned rosy-finches breed at an altitude that may be higher than that of any other North American bird. They hide their nest among rocks in the alpine tundra.

THE MOUNTAIN CLIMBER

Few animals are as equipped for alpine heights as the **mountain goat.** The two distinct layers of its winter coat help it stay warm on windy mountaintops, and its white coloring camouflages it against the snow. Its hooves spread wide for balance as it climbs, while the rough pads at the tips of its toes offer grip.

FORAGING
EDIBLE BOUQUETS

Pika don't hibernate, so they spend the brief alpine summer gathering enough food to eat over the winter. They make up to 100 trips a day between their burrow and the meadow, bringing back as much grass and flowers as they can carry in their mouths.

A pika may look like a rodent, but it's actually a very small relative of rabbits and hares.

UNIFORM
SEASONAL WARDROBE

The brown, spotted feathers of the **white-tailed ptarmigan's** summer coat help it camouflage among the rocks.

DOWN THE MOUNTAIN

Below the alpine tundra, a patchwork of pine forests, open meadows, and wetlands provide some of the richest habitats on the mountainside.

HUNTING
LION OF THE MOUNTAINS

One of the most athletic hunters in the Rockies, the **mountain lion** can leap a distance of 40 feet in a single bound, or jump 18 feet vertically up a tree.

The mountain lion goes by many other names, including puma, cougar, panther, and catamount (from "cat of the mountain").

UNIFORM
FLASHING RED

As part of its courtship display, the **dusky grouse** shows off the dark-red patches of skin on its neck sac as it hoots, struts, and fans its tail feathers.

UNIFORM
FRAGRANCE-FREE

The spotted coat of the baby **elk** helps it hide among the tall grasses of the meadow where it's born. It's also born with no scent, making it harder for predators to find it.

The rufous hummingbird travels down the Rockies in late summer and early fall, refueling on blooming wildflowers. Follow its migration route to page 49.

CRASH HELMET

Bighorn sheep rams knock heads to establish dominance, colliding at a speed of 30 miles per hour and creating an impact that can be heard up to a mile away. Two layers of bone beneath their horns help protect their brains.

ATHLETICS

THE DIVING DEER

Moose swim to cool off on warm days, avoid insects, or feed on aquatic plants. They can even dive up to 20 feet to browse at the bottoms of lakes and ponds!

HUNTING

CHILD PRODIGIES

Though the chicks of the **common merganser** stay close to their mother, they're able to hunt for themselves within a day of hatching. They start by eating aquatic insects, moving on to fish at 12 days old.

FIELD SIGNALS

SLAP SIGNALS

Beavers slap the surface of the water with their wide, flat tail to warn their family of danger.

PONDEROSAS AND PIÑÓNS

Among the lower slopes and foothills of the Southern Rockies, forests of towering ponderosa pines transition to scrubby piñón–juniper woodland at the edge of the southwestern desert.

SHELTER
DINING AT HOME

The **Abert's squirrel** builds big, messy nests in ponderosa pines. The trees are also their food source: the squirrel eats pine cones, twigs, and buds.

TOOLKIT
TWO-PURPOSE TAIL

The top of the **North American porcupine's** tail is covered in quills that can be used in defense against predators, while the bottom has bristle-like hairs that help it climb trees.

FORAGING
A BEAK FOR BARK

Pygmy nuthatches hop up and down ponderosas, using their thin beaks to probe for insects and spiders or to store seeds under the bark to eat later.

UNIFORM
THE HUNTER'S CAMOUFLAGE

The **poorwill** waits for insects on the ground, where its mottled coat helps it hide among the rocky foothill slopes.

FORAGING
EATING THE LEFTOVERS

Mule deer can't reach high enough to eat the more delicate upper twigs of the ponderosa pine, so they wait to eat the ones dropped by the Abert's squirrel.

pinyon jay

FORAGING
BERRIES AND SEEDS

Growing in the arid landscape at the meeting place of mountain and desert, the seeds from piñóns and the berries from juniper trees are important food sources for a variety of animals.

western bluebird

As omnivores, gray foxes supplement the meat in their diets with berries and nuts.

ATHLETICS
THE CLIMBING CANID

Gray foxes are the only species of canine in North America that can climb trees, thanks to their unique arms. Their forearms rotate less like a dog's and more like a cat's or a bear's.

FIELD SIGNALS
HEAD BUMP

Bobcats bump their heads in greeting, trading signals from their scent glands.

cliff chipmunk

striped skunk

HUNTING
THRASHER

Roadrunners are skilled hunters and can even take on rattlesnakes, swinging them against rocks to kill them before the snake can strike.

Piñón–juniper woodlands grow on many of the mountains scattered across the desert between the Rockies and the Eastern Sierras (page 86).

LA FRONTERA

Throughout the borderlands, forested mountains rise above the arid desert, providing a refuge for animals crossing between Mexico and the United States.

SURVIVALISTS
BORDER CAT

Jaguars used to roam as far north as the Grand Canyon, but they were hunted to extinction in the United States by the 1960s. They still live in the mountains of northern Mexico, and in recent years some brave jaguars have crossed into Arizona and New Mexico in search of new hunting grounds.

NAVIGATION
CAVERN COLONIES

An opening into the earth beneath the Guadalupe Mountains, the cool, dark interior of Carlsbad Caverns provides a summer home for two different species that migrate from Central America.

Cave swallows return to the United States in February. Using mud and bat guano, they build their nests near the cavern's entrance.

From April to October, Mexican free-tailed bats roost in Carlsbad Caverns in groups of up to 400,000. They emerge together at dusk to feed, appearing as a huge, swirling cloud.

FIELD SIGNALS
SHARED LANGUAGE

Some animals prefer to navigate the wilderness in a group. To keep track of each other, they use a variety of communication methods, including sound, scent, and body language.

The smallest and rarest subspecies of gray wolves, lobos (Mexican gray wolves) live in packs made up of a breeding pair and their offspring. Their howl, which can be heard for miles, is used to rally the pack.

Javelinas live in groups called squadrons. They communicate by clacking their tusks together and through scent marking.

Female white-nosed coati travel with their young through mountain canyons in large bands, using their tails to signal to one another. Tails straight up mean all is well; tails held down warn of danger.

INTO THE DESERT

The largest desert in North America, most of the Chihuahuan Desert spreads across central Mexico, but its northern boundaries stretch into Texas, New Mexico, and Arizona. Animals that live in this high-altitude desert must survive scorching summers, chilling winters, and long stretches of time between rain.

FIELD SIGNALS

DESERT BALLAD

Coyotes yip and sing together from across the desert, announcing their presence and helping family members locate one other.

SHELTER

DEVELOPER OF THE DIRT

The **American badger's** muscular legs and long claws allow them to dig into the compacted desert soil. Many different animals rely on the abandoned burrows they leave behind for shelter.

Burrows stay cool in the summer, warm in the winter, and retain humidity inside.

HUNTING

AN ALLURING FRAGRANCE

Burrowing owls collect the dung of other animals, scattering it in and around their homes. The scent attracts beetles, the owl's favorite prey.

When threatened, burrowing owls make a screeching hiss that may mimic the sound of a rattlesnake.

HUNTING

GROUND BATTLE

Most predatory bats catch their meals in the air, but **pallid bats** stalk their prey on the ground, crawling over dirt and sand to grab scorpions, spiders, and even mice!

## OPEN WIDE

The **lesser nighthawk** flies through the air with its large mouth open, capturing flies, moths, and mosquitos.

In the winter, nighthawks migrate to Mexico and Central America.

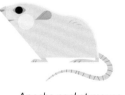

 ATHLETICS
HIGH JUMP

Despite having a body only a little over 3 inches long, **Merriam's kangaroo rats** can jump 9 feet in the air to evade predators.

 TOOLKIT
RUNNING SHOES

Fur between the **kit fox's** toes gives it extra traction on sand, enabling it to run at speeds of up to 25 miles per hour.

 UNIFORM
BRIGHTER WHITES

In southern New Mexico, eroding gypsum has created an area of white sand dunes. To better blend in, some animals have evolved to become lighter in color.

bleached earless lizard

sand-treader camel cricket

sand wolf spider

Apache pocket mouse

LAND OF THE SAGUARO

Far from being a barren wasteland, the Sonoran Desert is a rich and diverse ecosystem that is home to more than 2,000 species of flowering plants. Towering above this desert garden is the saguaro, the tallest cactus in the United States and a source of life for many Sonoran creatures.

lesser long-nosed bat

FORAGING

24-HOUR DINER

Saguaro flowers bloom at night and last for just one day. Their nectar feeds bats throughout the night and birds and insects the following morning.

HUNTING

INSECT ASSASSIN

The smallest owl in the world, the **elf owl** hunts for crickets, beetles, and spiders.

ATHLETICS

HANDSTAND

To warn off predators, the **spotted skunk** stands on its hands and lifts its tail in the air.

HUNTING

SCORPION HUNTER

The **grasshopper mouse** is able to hunt for scorpions because it has evolved to be resistant to the toxins in their sting.

Grasshopper mice "howl" to defend their territory.

FORAGING

LATE-NIGHT SNACKING

Usually active during the day, **gila monsters** become more nocturnal during the hottest part of the summer, when they'll emerge at night to feast on eggs and small birds.

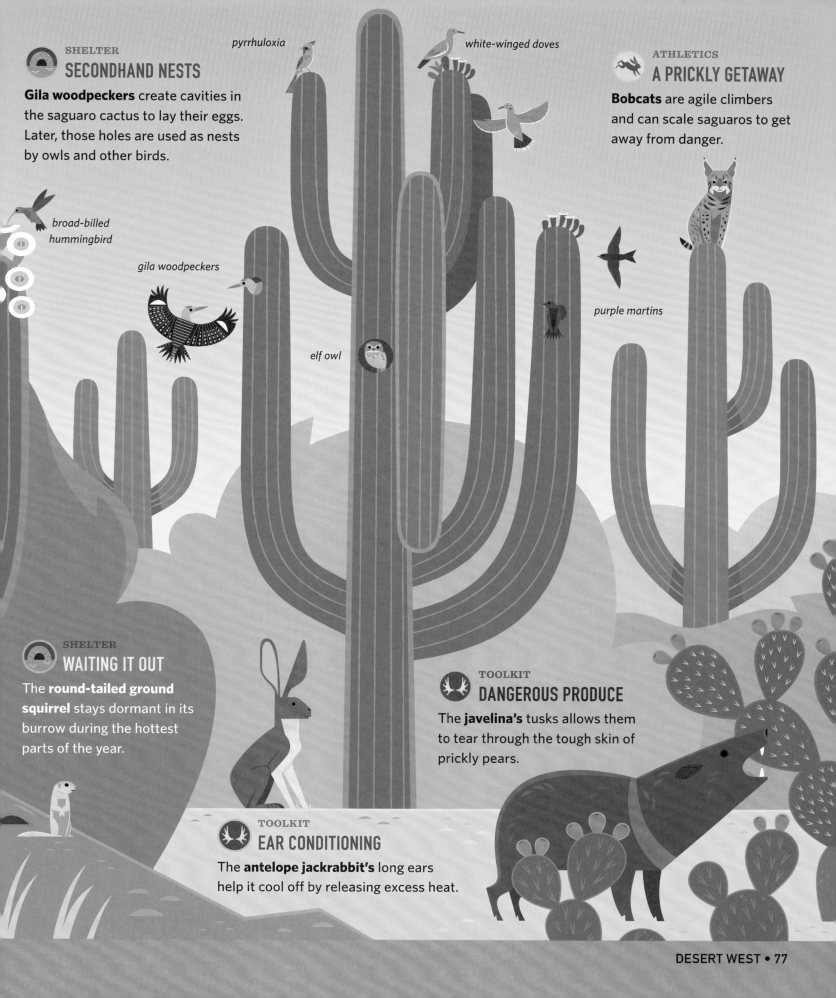

SHELTER
SECONDHAND NESTS

Gila woodpeckers create cavities in the saguaro cactus to lay their eggs. Later, those holes are used as nests by owls and other birds.

pyrrhuloxia

white-winged doves

ATHLETICS
A PRICKLY GETAWAY

Bobcats are agile climbers and can scale saguaros to get away from danger.

broad-billed hummingbird

gila woodpeckers

elf owl

purple martins

SHELTER
WAITING IT OUT

The **round-tailed ground squirrel** stays dormant in its burrow during the hottest parts of the year.

TOOLKIT
DANGEROUS PRODUCE

The **javelina's** tusks allows them to tear through the tough skin of prickly pears.

TOOLKIT
EAR CONDITIONING

The **antelope jackrabbit's** long ears help it cool off by releasing excess heat.

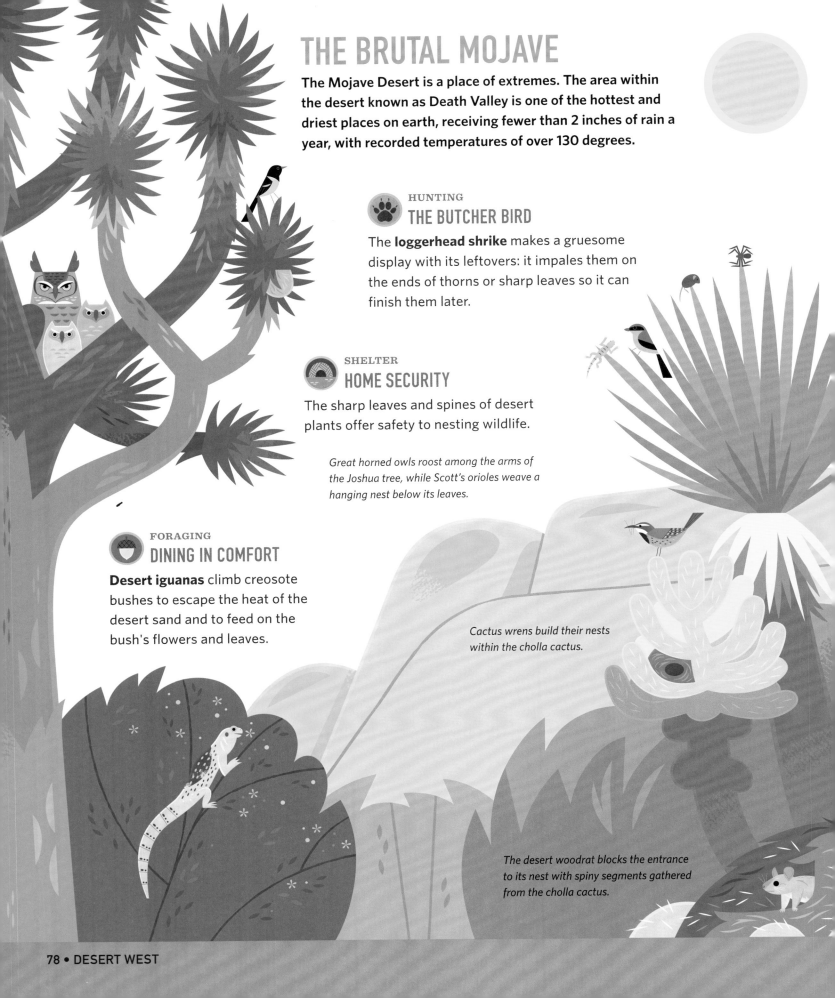

THE BRUTAL MOJAVE

The Mojave Desert is a place of extremes. The area within the desert known as Death Valley is one of the hottest and driest places on earth, receiving fewer than 2 inches of rain a year, with recorded temperatures of over 130 degrees.

HUNTING
THE BUTCHER BIRD

The **loggerhead shrike** makes a gruesome display with its leftovers: it impales them on the ends of thorns or sharp leaves so it can finish them later.

SHELTER
HOME SECURITY

The sharp leaves and spines of desert plants offer safety to nesting wildlife.

Great horned owls roost among the arms of the Joshua tree, while Scott's orioles weave a hanging nest below its leaves.

FORAGING
DINING IN COMFORT

Desert iguanas climb creosote bushes to escape the heat of the desert sand and to feed on the bush's flowers and leaves.

Cactus wrens build their nests within the cholla cactus.

The desert woodrat blocks the entrance to its nest with spiny segments gathered from the cholla cactus.

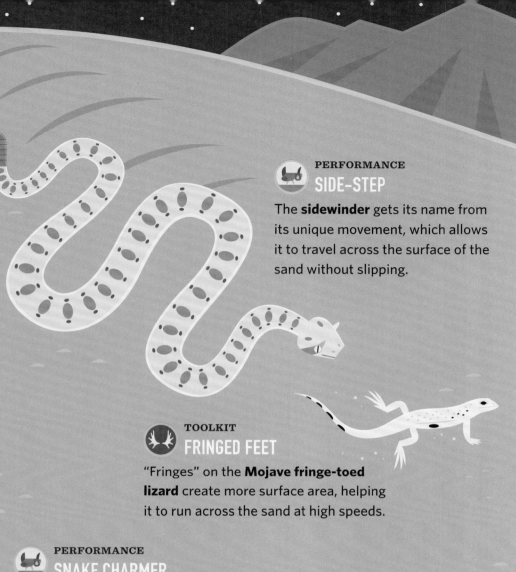

PERFORMANCE
SIDE-STEP

The **sidewinder** gets its name from its unique movement, which allows it to travel across the surface of the sand without slipping.

TOOLKIT
FRINGED FEET

"Fringes" on the **Mojave fringe-toed lizard** create more surface area, helping it to run across the sand at high speeds.

PERFORMANCE
SNAKE CHARMER

The **desert kangaroo rat** has an unusual method to avoid getting attacked by a rattlesnake: it dances. It jumps backward, drums its feet, and kicks up sand, showing the snake that it's too fast and agile to be worth trying to catch.

Western diamondback rattlesnakes can grow up to 7 feet long!

TOOLKIT
COLD-BLOODED DEFENSES

As reptiles, lizards need to spend time in the sun warming up, leaving them exposed to danger. To protect themselves, desert lizards have evolved a variety of defense methods.

The zebra-tailed lizard whips its striped tail back and forth to distract predators.

The gila monster can release venom with its bite.

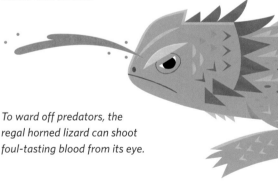

To ward off predators, the regal horned lizard can shoot foul-tasting blood from its eye.

The chuckwalla hides in rock crevices, puffing out its body so that it's impossible to dislodge.

DESERT RAIN

Rain transforms the Chihuahuan, Sonoran, and Mojave deserts. Animals that have stayed hidden over the long, dry months now emerge, traveling to temporary pools to drink, bathe, and lay their eggs. Succulents store up moisture so they may survive another year. And the rains bring another gift: wildflowers that briefly blaze across the desert.

ATHLETICS
TORTOISE KNOCKOUT

When two male **desert tortoises** meet, they may wrestle for dominance, each trying to flip the other over.

TOOLKIT
SELF STORAGE

During the dry season, **gila monsters** survive off the fat stored in their tails.

TOOLKIT
DEFENSE SYSTEMS

Drawn out of their hiding places by the rain, some animals have defenses to keep themselves safe. The **Sonoran desert toad** has a toxin that coats its skin, while the slow-moving **rosy boa** can release a foul musk to ward off predators.

Spadefoots bury themselves in the ground during the dry season, emerging once they feel the vibrations of thunder.

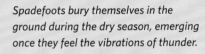

FIELD SIGNALS
BAA, BAA SPADEFOOT

During the monsoon, **Couch's spadefoots** emerge to mate in temporary pools of rainwater. To attract a female, male spadefoots make a call that sounds like the bleating of a sheep or a goat.

Spadefoot tadpoles hatch quickly and can metamorphose into froglets in as few as 9 days, racing to beat the drying up of their pool.

A BRIEFLY BLOOMING BOUQUET

Monsoon season can turn even the most arid desert into a meadow of boldly colored wildflowers, offering animals a brief opportunity to feed on pollen and nectar.

Ocotillo bloom every year, making them a reliable source of nectar for hummingbirds and carpenter bees.

Long-tongued bats migrate from Mexico into the United States following the blooming of agaves, which sustain them along their travels.

Costa's hummingbird

The rufous hummingbird feeds on ocotillo while traveling north out of Mexico. Follow it to page 91.

Mojave wildflowers that have lain dormant throughout the year bloom in the spring, providing a feast for bees, butterflies, and desert tortoises.

Hawk moths use their long, hollow tongues to reach the nectar deep inside the night-blooming cereus, a cactus whose flowers all open at the same time and last for only a single night.

A DEADLY DANCE

The male **desert tarantula** emerges during the summer rains to search for a mate. He taps at the entrance of a female's burrow to draw her out, then performs a dance. If she isn't impressed, she may eat him and wait for another suitor.

CANYONLANDS

Carved over millions of years by wind and water, a maze of canyons offers a hideout from both predators and the desert heat.

The bighorn's wide-set eyes help it to watch for predators.

The desert bighorn ram can go up to a week without drinking water.

WILDERNESS EXPERTS

KING OF THE CLIFFS

Canyons provide the perfect refuge for the **desert bighorn sheep**. They can quickly scramble up sheer cliffs and rocky outcrops that predators can't climb, giving them a vertical escape route from danger. They use their excellent eyesight to judge distances, helping them jump over canyons and ravines, and their padded hooves help cushion their landing.

A California condor glides far above the canyon. Soar with it to the Pacific Coast on page 88.

A bighorn can perch on a le that's only 2 inches wide!

SHELTER
A ROCKY ROOST

Mexican spotted owls usually like to roost in trees, but here in the desert, where trees can be hard to find, they sometimes roost on ledges along canyon walls.

FORAGING
CUPBOARD IN THE CLIFFS

Cliff chipmunks store juniper berries and piñón seeds in the deep rock crevices where they live.

ATHLETICS
DESERT ACROBAT

The **ring-tailed cat** is an agile climber. With ankles that rotate 180 degrees and a long tail to provide balance, it scales trees and cliffs with ease.

UNIFORM
THE INVISIBLE AMPHIBIAN

A **canyon tree frog's** skin is colored to match its rocky home, which helps it blend in with the cliffs and stone crevices where it lives.

THE SAGEBRUSH STEPPE

An immense high-altitude desert between the Rockies and the Sierra Nevadas, the Great Basin is dominated by a single plant: the sagebrush. A hardy, woody shrub, it provides shelter and food to the animals of the region, even in the coldest months of winter.

PERFORMANCE
BOOM, BOOM

As dawn breaks on an early spring morning, the male **greater sage grouse** steps onto its lek to begin its courtship display. It struts, fans its feathers, and makes a loud booming call using the air sacs in its chest. Females will compare the performances of different males before making a selection.

NAVIGATION
COMING DOWN THE MOUNTAIN

Many smaller birds leave the sagebrush steppe in the winter, but for the **gray-crowned rosy-finch**, the Great Basin is a winter escape from the heavy snow of the Rocky Mountains.

Follow the rosy-finch back up the mountain to its nesting site on page 66.

FORAGING
FRESH SAGE

Some animals on the steppe have developed a resistance to the toxic chemicals in sagebrush, giving them a reliable food source in the winter, when little else is growing.

sage grouse hen

White-tailed prairie dogs hibernate for most of the winter. When they emerge, they'll survive on sagebrush until dandelions and grasses begin to grow.

COMMUNITY
COZYING UP

Great Basin rattlesnakes hibernate over winter. Finding a good den can be difficult on the steppe, so they often share.

Though commonly called an antelope, pronghorns are a unique species that are more closely related to giraffes.

HUNTING
AN UNLIKELY TEAM

Coyotes and **American badgers** work together to hunt ground squirrels. While the badger digs in through one burrow entrance, the coyote waits at the other: whichever way the rodent goes, one of the predators gets a meal.

SHELTER
UNDER THE SAGEBRUSH

The **pygmy rabbit** spends winter under the sagebrush, tunneling through the snow to eat from other bushes.

The smallest rabbit in the world, the pygmy rabbit measures less than a foot long.

FIELD SIGNALS
SCENTING A MESSAGE

When a **pronghorn** senses danger, it raises the white fur around its tail and releases a warning odor to alert its herd.

SHELTER
KEEP THE DOOR CLOSED

The **Ord's kangaroo rat** spends the day in its shallow, underground burrow. It plugs the entrance with dirt to keep in moisture and maintain a comfortable temperature.

THE SIERRA NEVADAS

As rain-bearing winds travel inland from the Pacific Ocean, they're blocked by the Sierra Nevada Mountains. This creates a rain shadow effect, splitting the two sides of the mountain range into very different worlds.

THE EASTERN SIERRAS

The Sierra Nevada Mountains rise from the edge of the arid Mojave and Great Basin Deserts.

Sierra Nevada bighorn can be told apart from other bighorns by their wide, flaring horns.

SURVIVALISTS
RAREST OF THE BIGHORNS

The last remaining **Sierra Nevada bighorns** graze among the alpine peaks.

NAVIGATION
FOLLOWING THE FOOD

Mule deer in the Eastern Sierras winter in the snow-free valleys, searching among the sagebrush for food. After the spring melt, they climb to forage on more nutritious high-altitude plants.

TOOLKIT
A HIDDEN POCKET

The **Clark's nutcracker** gathers seeds from the bristlecone pine, using the pouch under its tongue to carry up to 150 seeds at a time to store for later.

American avocet

A Wilson's phalarope may triple its weight at Mono Lake before continuing on to South America.

FORAGING
A DRY SPELL

The **panamint chipmunk** survives without drinking water by getting all the moisture it needs from the seeds and lichens it eats.

FORAGING
SHRIMP FEST

Mono Lake is too saline for fish, but its population of **brine shrimp** and **alkali flies** draws millions of migratory shorebirds.

eared grebe

THE WESTERN SIERRAS

On the mountain's western slopes, rain and fog from the Pacific Ocean nourish forests where the largest trees in the world grow.

SHELTER
HOME FURNISHING

Western gray squirrels shred the sequoia's bark for material to line their nests.

UNIFORM
MOUNTAIN PARKA

The rare **Sierra Nevada red fox** lives at a much higher elevation than other red foxes, so it has a particularly full winter coat to help it stay warm.

NAVIGATION
TAKING THE LOW ROAD

Mountain quail spend spring and summer at elevations of up to 10,000 feet, moving downhill in winter to escape the snow.

HUNTING
A ROYAL RECLUSE

The secretive **mountain kingsnake** lives among rock crevices, emerging to hunt for lizards and nesting birds.

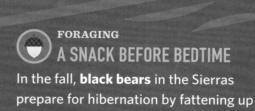

Black bears in the Sierras are usually cinnamon colored.

FORAGING
A SNACK BEFORE BEDTIME

In the fall, **black bears** in the Sierras prepare for hibernation by fattening up on acorns, berries, and nuts.

FORAGING
ACCIDENTAL ARBORIST

Douglas squirrels store sequoia pine cones to eat later, helping to spread their seeds throughout the forest.

THE MAMMOTH BIRD

California condors flourished during the Pleistocene, when they ranged as far east as New York and Florida and fed on the remains of megafauna like mammoths and giant ground sloths. When these creatures went extinct, the condor's range began to shrink. This process was accelerated in recent decades as human-made poisons were introduced into their diet, nearly leading to the extinction of these incredible birds.

Condors lay their eggs in cliffside caves or in tree cavities high in coastal redwoods (page 99). In the past, condors have nested in giant sequoia as well. They generally only have one chick every two years.

SURVIVALISTS
BACK FROM THE BRINK

By 1981 there were only 22 **California condors** left in the wild. Conservationists worked to trap all of the remaining birds so that they could start a captive breeding program. Captive-bred condors were gradually reintroduced to the wild, where they continued to be closely monitored. Thanks to these conservation efforts, California condors are once again soaring across the American West.

Condors can soar for hours at a time, riding air currents to heights of up to 15,000 feet.

With a wingspan of nearly 10 feet, the California condor is the largest bird in North America and the second-largest flying bird in the world after the Andean condor.

Juvenile condors are almost entirely black. Their heads become colorful as adults, at six to eight years old.

During courtship, condors present their wings and preen each other's feathers.

THE CHAPARRAL

The chaparral is an arid landscape shaped by long droughts and frequent wildfires. Deep-rooted grasses and shrubs grow back quickly after a blaze, while trees grow back much more slowly, creating a mosaic of oak woodlands, sagebrush scrub, and open grasslands.

HUNTING

CHAPARRAL CAT

Bobcats prowl the brushy chaparral, using their excellent hearing, sight, and sense of smell to locate small prey.

FORAGING

CUSTOM CABINETRY

The **acorn woodpecker** stores nuts in a central granary, drilling holes in dead trees fitted to the size of the individual acorns it gathers.

FORAGING

A HEALTHY GUT

During periods of drought, **California quails** get all of the water they need from the plants and insects they eat. Protozoans in their intestines help them digest plant matter.

NAVIGATION

BACK ON DRY LAND

Western pond turtles move back and forth between their terrestrial and aquatic habitats throughout the year. They feed only in the water but lay their eggs and overwinter on land, spending most of the year out of the water.

TOOLKIT

THE THRASHER'S BILL

The **California thrasher** uses its long, curved beak to flip through leaves as it seeks out insects, spiders, and grubs.

ATHLETICS
ARBOREAL AMPHIBIAN

Arboreal salamanders spend most of their time in the leaf litter, but their large toes and prehensile tails allow them to climb oaks and pines to find tree cavities where they can lay their eggs or wait out dry months.

FIELD SIGNALS
WIND INSTRUMENTS

During its courtship display, the **Allen's hummingbird** dives at a high speed, using the vibrations of air against its tail feathers to make two different notes.

The rufous hummingbird travels through California in the spring as it heads north. Follow it to its nesting site on page 108.

UNIFORM
SPOTS TO GROW OUT OF

Unlike their mostly solid-colored parents, **mountain lion** cubs are born covered in dark spots, which help them stay hidden on the shadowy forest floor when their mother is out hunting.

FIELD SIGNALS
DRUMROLL

By rapidly tapping their hind feet, **giant kangaroo rats** send messages to claim territory, express their mating status, and identify themselves.

HUNTING
ALLIGATOR OF THE WEST

Southern alligator lizards hunt for beetles, grasshoppers, and crickets and will sometimes even eat young mammals and birds.

SAND AND SURF

At the edge of the Pacific Ocean, wildlife living along the shoreline face a unique set of obstacles, from the exposure of nesting on the open beach to the challenges of living in the shallow and unpredictable surf.

PERFORMANCE
A PREDATOR PLAY

A mother **killdeer** digs a shallow nest right on the ground. To protect her young, she pretends that her wing is injured, making herself look like an easy target to draw predators away from her nest.

black-necked stilt

SURVIVALISTS
THE SHOVELNOSE

A member of the ray family, the **shovelnose guitarfish** has been around in nearly the same form for 100 million years!

TOOLKIT
ADDING BALLAST

Pacific sand dollars stand up in the water to feed and lie flat when the current is rough. Young sand dollars will swallow sand to help weigh themselves down.

HUNTING
EYES OUT

With both eyes on the same side of its body, the **California halibut** is able to bury itself flat in the sand while still keeping watch for a meal.

UNIFORM
DRESSED FOR THE BEACH

Snowy plovers nest right on the beach dunes, where both their eggs and their chicks are camouflaged to blend in with the sand.

Snowy plover chicks leave the nest within hours of hatching, following their parents to feeding sites.

Though plover chicks have small bodies, their legs are already the height of a full-grown adult's.

FORAGING
SURF AND TURF

With only their faces exposed, **sand crabs** dig backward into the sand at the spot where the surf breaks on the shore. They filter plankton out of the water with their antennae as waves rush past.

UNIFORM
WIDE-EYED

The eyespots on the **big skate's** fins may help confuse predators.

TOOLKIT
A BEAK FOR EVERY PURPOSE

The beaks of shorebirds come in very unusual forms, allowing them to feed on different aquatic prey.

The black-necked stilt uses its long bill to peck insects, crayfish, and small fish out of the water.

The black oystercatcher has a strong, straight bill to pry open mussels and limpets.

The American avocet sweeps its long, curved beak through the water to find shrimp and aquatic insects.

The black skimmer flies low over the water, using the longer, lower part of its beak to skim for prey.

PACIFIC PREDATORS

Beneath the deceptively calm surface of the Pacific Ocean, aquatic hunters of all shapes and sizes are busy pursuing prey.

COMMUNITY
SWIM TEAM

The highly social **short-beaked common dolphin** can live and hunt in pods of several thousands.

HUNTING
THE LITTLE HUNTER

Harbor porpoises hunt in bays and inlets for small fish, eating 10 percent of their body weight each day.

ATHLETICS
A MARINE MARATHON

California sea lions can swim at over 25 miles per hour and can hunt for up to 30 hours continuously.

SURVIVALISTS
THE LOST COLONY

Guadalupe fur seals were considered extinct until a small population was discovered off Mexico in the 1950s.

TOOLKIT
ON THE SCENT

The **red octopus** has thousands of receptors on its tentacles that help it track down prey on the sandy seafloor.

NAVIGATION
RIVER GIANT

White sturgeon hunt the estuary floor for clams, worms, and mussels. They don't mature until they are more than fifteen years old, at which point they can travel upstream to spawn.

Measuring up to 20 feet, white sturgeons are the largest freshwater fish in North America.

The marbled murrelet forages for small fish in the shallow waters close to shore. Follow this one to her surprising nesting site on page 99.

HUNTING
THE GREAT WHITE

Great white sharks are able to smell a colony of seals from 2 miles away.

Follow the great white shark across the ocean to its other hunting grounds on page 117.

UNIFORM
WET SUIT

The feathers of the **Brandt's cormorant** aren't fully waterproof, which makes them less buoyant when wet, allowing cormorants to dive up to 230 feet. After diving, they dry off in the sun (page 97).

COMMUNITY
PACK HUNTERS

By working together in packs, **transient orcas** are able to skillfully hunt seals and sea lions and even pursue large prey, like young whales.

THE CHANNEL ISLANDS

Located along migration routes off the coast of California, the Channel Islands' isolated beaches and peaceful waters welcome species from throughout the Pacific. Far less mobile, the islands' land-dwelling species live stranded in isolation, creating a laboratory for evolution.

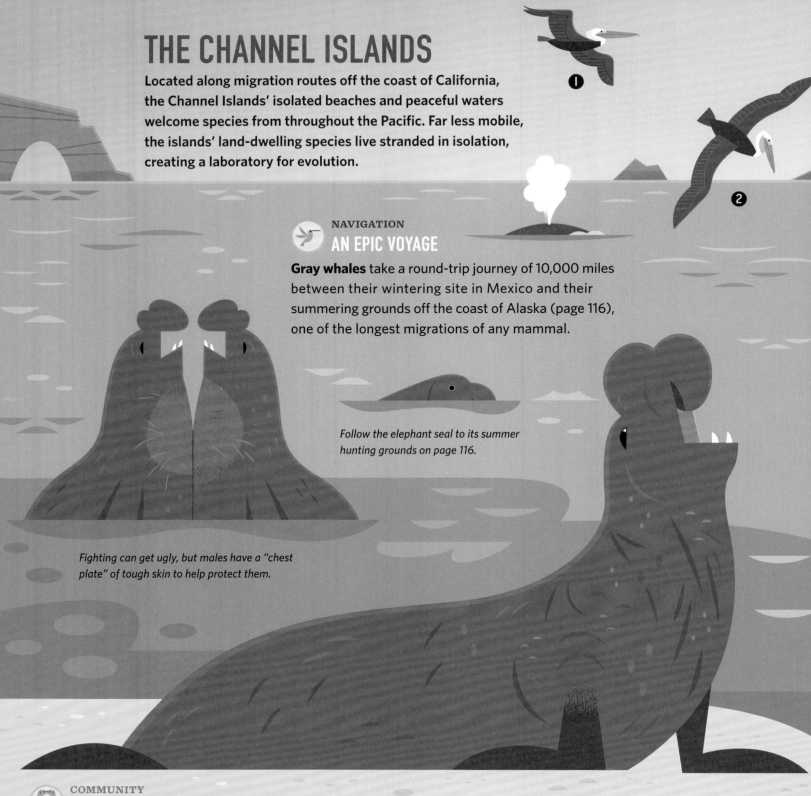

NAVIGATION
AN EPIC VOYAGE

Gray whales take a round-trip journey of 10,000 miles between their wintering site in Mexico and their summering grounds off the coast of Alaska (page 116), one of the longest migrations of any mammal.

Follow the elephant seal to its summer hunting grounds on page 116.

Fighting can get ugly, but males have a "chest plate" of tough skin to help protect them.

COMMUNITY
AMERICAN ELEPHANTS

Northern elephant seals spend 90 percent of their time at sea, where they hunt for deepwater fish and mollusks. Adult males return to shore in December, fighting one another to claim territory on the beach. Females follow shortly after, joining the territory of the males who won their battles.

Male elephant seals can weigh up to 5,000 pounds! They use their long, floppy noses to make a loud, drum-like sound to drive away their rivals.

Laysan albatross

SOUNDS OF HOME

The rookery of the **California sea lion** is a very noisy place. Bulls defend their territory with a loud bark, while pups find their mothers by following the unique sound of her voice.

Brandt's cormorants

HUNTING
CATCH OF THE DAY

To grab a meal, **brown pelicans** combine their keen eyesight, daring flight abilities, and unique anatomy.

1. *The pelican spots fish while flying overhead.*
2. *It plunges up to 70 feet down.*
3. *It rises with a bill full of fish and water.*

Jays that live in pine forests have longer beaks, so they can pry open pine cones.

SURVIVALISTS
ISLAND FOX

A descendent of the gray fox (page 71), the **island fox** is isolated to the Channel Islands, where it has evolved to become smaller over time. At 19 inches long and 4 pounds, they are one of the most diminuitive canids in the world. Changes in the island ecosystem nearly led to their extinction, but conservationists have helped them recover.

Jays that live in oak forests have a short, blunt bill, which helps them eat acorns.

TOOLKIT
GROWING APART

Since settling in the Channel Islands, **island scrub jays** have gradually become one-third larger than their mainland relatives. And though they all live on the same island, they've evolved into two different groups, each with a uniquely shaped beak.

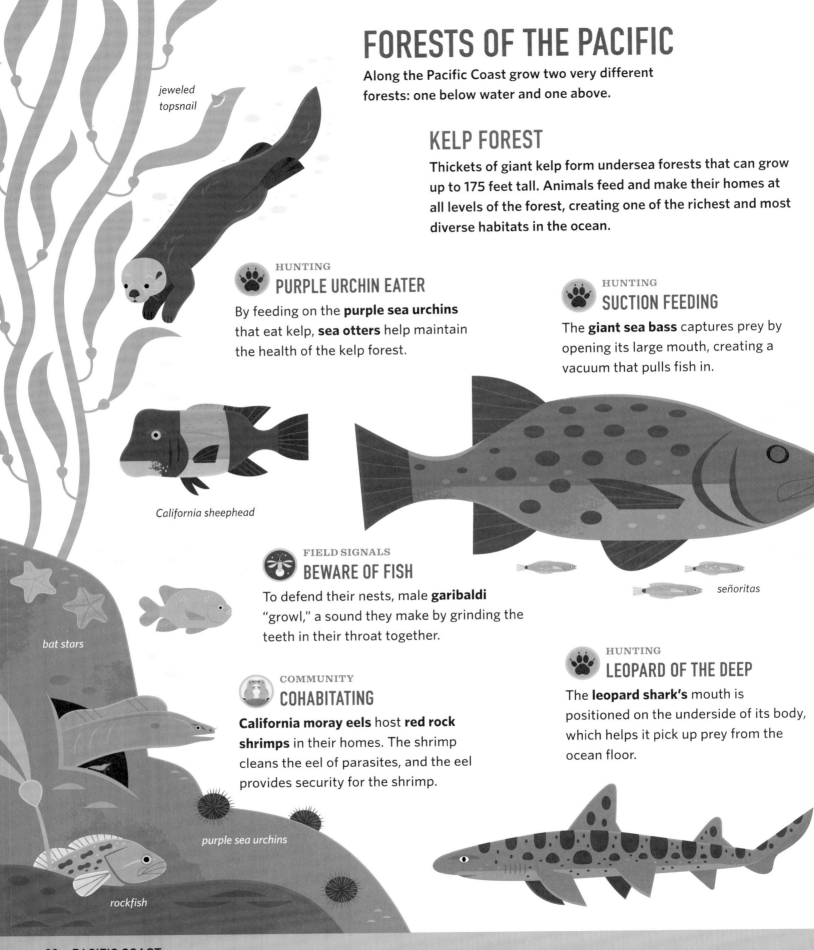

FORESTS OF THE PACIFIC

Along the Pacific Coast grow two very different forests: one below water and one above.

jeweled topsnail

KELP FOREST

Thickets of giant kelp form undersea forests that can grow up to 175 feet tall. Animals feed and make their homes at all levels of the forest, creating one of the richest and most diverse habitats in the ocean.

HUNTING
PURPLE URCHIN EATER

By feeding on the **purple sea urchins** that eat kelp, **sea otters** help maintain the health of the kelp forest.

HUNTING
SUCTION FEEDING

The **giant sea bass** captures prey by opening its large mouth, creating a vacuum that pulls fish in.

California sheephead

señoritas

FIELD SIGNALS
BEWARE OF FISH

To defend their nests, male **garibaldi** "growl," a sound they make by grinding the teeth in their throat together.

bat stars

HUNTING
LEOPARD OF THE DEEP

The **leopard shark's** mouth is positioned on the underside of its body, which helps it pick up prey from the ocean floor.

COMMUNITY
COHABITATING

California moray eels host **red rock shrimps** in their homes. The shrimp cleans the eel of parasites, and the eel provides security for the shrimp.

purple sea urchins

rockfish

REDWOOD FOREST

The moist ocean air drifts to the coast, where it nurtures the tallest trees in the world: Pacific redwoods, which can soar to over 350 feet tall. High in their canopy is a mysterious world few will ever see.

SHELTER
THE MYSTERIOUS NEST

For many years, no one knew where the **marbled murrelet** nested. It forages at sea but nests deep in the forest on branches 150 feet above the ground. Instead of building a nest, it simply lays its eggs among lichen and moss.

red tree vole

HUNTING
HUNTING THE HEIGHTS

Wandering salamanders hunt the canopy for tiny arboreal crustaceans.

little brown bat

SHELTER
THIS OLD TREE HOUSE

Pacific redwoods can live to be over two thousand years old, their trunks typically scarred over time by fire damage and decay. This creates cavities, which a variety of creatures use as nests.

Humboldt flying squirrels

FIELD SIGNALS
FEELING TALKATIVE

Steller's jays fill the forest with noise. They chirp, whistle, and even imitate squirrels, hawks, and other birds.

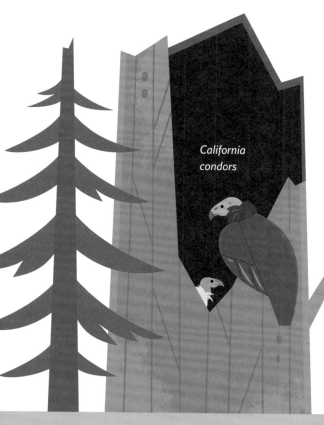

California condors

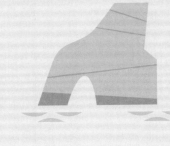

SHIFTING SHORES

The worlds of sea and land are never truly separated along the coast, particularly in the Pacific Northwest. Receding tides leave pools brimming with marine life, forest animals forage along the beach, and fish leave the ocean to migrate upriver.

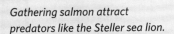

 TOOLKIT
SEAFOOD MALLET

Sea otters crack shells using small rocks and will pound mussels against larger stones to get them open.

Gathering salmon attract predators like the Steller sea lion.

Salmon follow their strong sense of smell to locate the tributary of the river where they were born.

 TOOLKIT
SUPERGLUE

To stand up to waves and resist the pull of the tide, **mussels** create an incredibly strong adhesive out of of proteins, keeping them secured to the rocks where they live.

 HUNTING
STEALTH HUNTERS

Sea stars are slow-moving hunters that have a big impact on tide pools. By eating mussels, they clear room for anemones and other creatures.

 FORAGING
SIDE OF GREENS

The **green sea anemone** hunts for fish and crustaceans, but it also gets nutrition from the algae plants that grow inside it.

SURVIVALISTS
PRESIDENTIAL PROTECTION

The largest subspecies of elk, **Roosevelt elk**, were hunted nearly to extinction by the early 1900s. To help protect them, Teddy Roosevelt designated their habitat on the Olympic Peninsula a national monument in 1909.

western gull

NAVIGATION
THE LONG JOURNEY HOME

Pacific salmon hatch in freshwater, then travel downriver to spend their lives in the open ocean. After living at sea for several years, they begin a return journey back to the place of their birth, where they will lay their eggs. It is an incredible trek upstream and a yearly event that shapes life for all the animals who live in the region.

FORAGING
SEAFOOD BUFFET

Trapped away from the ocean, tidal pools offer foraging for animals like **black bears**, **raccoons**, and **gulls**.

SHELTER
AT HOME IN THE DAMP

Despite its name, the **mountain beaver** is not a beaver, and it doesn't live primarily in the mountains. A unique burrowing rodent, the mountain beaver needs to drink one-third of its own body weight each day to survive, so it digs its home in humid forests.

HUNTING
A GIANT APPETITE

Reaching up to 13 inches in length, **giant pacific salamanders** prowl along mountain streams and across the wet forest floor hunting for fish, rodents, and banana slugs.

LIFE AND DEATH IN THE RAINFOREST

Lacking the extreme seasons of the eastern woodlands or the frozen winters of the northern taiga, life in the temperate rainforest of the Pacific Coast is a continual cycle of growth and decay.

FORAGING
A ROTTING RESTAURANT

Hairy woodpeckers excavate rotting wood to find beetle larvae and other wood-boring insects.

FORAGING

CREATING COMPOST

Pacific banana slugs are detrivores, meaning they eat decaying plant matter. After processing it, they create nutrient-rich soil, fertilizing new plant life.

Able to grow up to 9 inches long, the Pacific banana slug is the second-largest slug in the world.

river otter

COMMUNITY

BACK TO THE LAND

Animals feed on **salmon** as they travel upstream, leaving their leftovers to rot. When an uneaten fish decomposes, it leaves behind nitrogen in the soil, which nourishes trees and plants, making salmon a vital part of the forest ecosystem.

Lampreys use their mouths to move rocks to build a nest for their eggs.

SURVIVALISTS
ANCIENT VOYAGERS

Like salmon, **Pacific lampreys** also migrate from the ocean to freshwater to spawn. A type of jawless fish, they have been around for 450 million years.

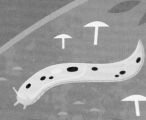

spotted owls

SHELTER
HOME, DEAD HOME

Snags, standing trees that are dead and decaying, serve an important role in forest life. Cavities created in their wood, either by rot or by woodpeckers, provide homes for birds and other animals.

Fishers hide their young in tree cavities, moving them to new dens as they outgrow their old ones.

ATHLETICS
FRESHWATER HURDLES

When **salmon** encounter waterfalls along their route, they have only one option: jump. They've been recorded leaping almost 12 feet vertically!

northern flicker

black bear

Brown creepers nest under the bark of dying trees.

If rivers are low, salmon must wait for rain to raise the water level so they can continue their journey upstream.

A rough-skinned newt's toxin is ten times more potent than cyanide.

TOOLKIT
ARMS RACE

Rough-skinned newts have developed one of the most potent toxins in the world to ward off predators, but **garter snakes** that live in their range have been able to develop a resistence.

SALMON RUN

The annual salmon migration is an event of incredible significance. This is true not only for the salmon that seek to spawn, but for the many other species that rely on the the salmon's arrival for their own survival.

bald eagle

glaucous-winged gull

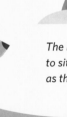

The bear's preferred method of fishing is to sit in deep water, waiting to grab fish as they swim past.

Some bears stand at the top of the waterfalls, hoping to catch fish in their mouths as they leap over.

 HUNTING
FISH MARKET

The salmon run is particularly important for Alaska's **coastal brown bears**, as it presents them with the ideal opportunity to build up their fat reserves as they prepare for hibernation. Brown bears gather at waterways along the salmon migration route each year, employing a variety of different methods to make their catch.

Salmon are so plentiful in season that bears often eat only the fattiest part of the fish, leaving the rest for scavengers like gulls and ravens.

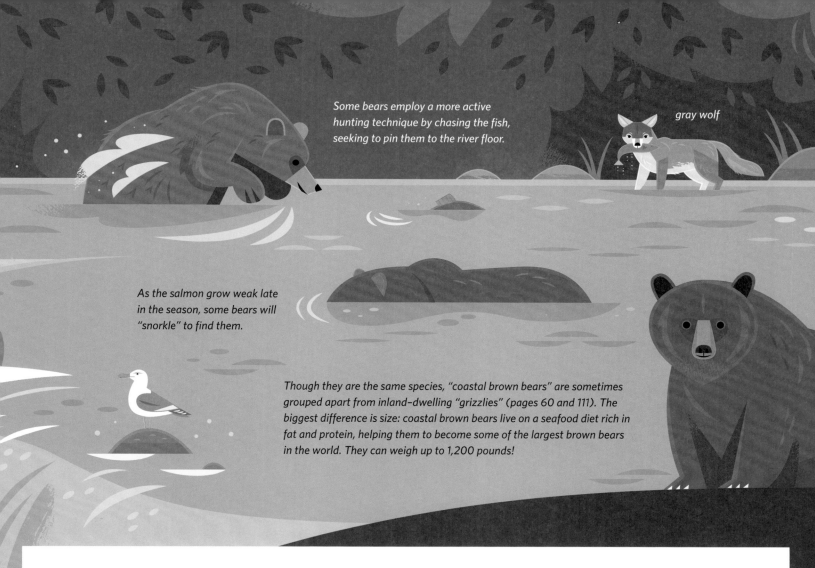

Some bears employ a more active hunting technique by chasing the fish, seeking to pin them to the river floor.

gray wolf

As the salmon grow weak late in the season, some bears will "snorkle" to find them.

Though they are the same species, "coastal brown bears" are sometimes grouped apart from inland–dwelling "grizzlies" (pages 60 and 111). The biggest difference is size: coastal brown bears live on a seafood diet rich in fat and protein, helping them to become some of the largest brown bears in the world. They can weigh up to 1,200 pounds!

IDENTIFICATION
PACIFIC SALMON

Five different species of **Pacific salmon** spawn in the United States. To make identification trickier, they transform as they travel upriver to spawn, changing their color and even altering the shape of their body.

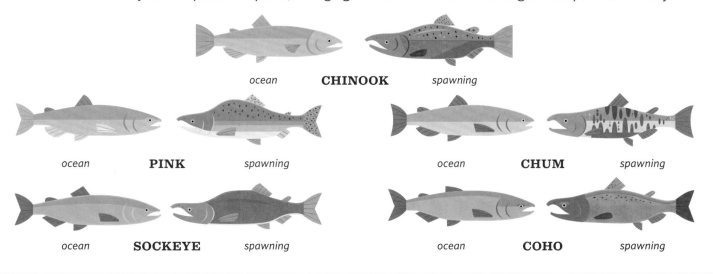

ocean	**CHINOOK**	spawning
ocean	**PINK**	spawning
ocean	**CHUM**	spawning
ocean	**SOCKEYE**	spawning
ocean	**COHO**	spawning

ISLANDS AND FJORDS

Alaska's southern coastline is a rocky landscape of towering offshore islands and winding fjords. Valleys carved by glaciers and filled with seawater, fjord estuaries are a unique ecosystem found only a few places on Earth.

HUNTING
BUBBLE NETS

Humpback whales travel from across the Pacific to feed along Alaska's coast in the summer. Working as a group, they employ a hunting technique called bubble net fishing. They circle schools of fish while blowing bubbles to create a "net" that traps the fish in its center.

Follow the humpback whales to their winter mating grounds on page 117.

Follow the humpback whales to their winter mating grounds on page 117.

UNIFORM
SAFETY SUIT

A thick coat of guard hairs help protect the **Steller sea lion's** skin when it hauls itself out onto jagged rocks to dry off.

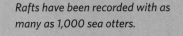

Rafts have been recorded with as many as 1,000 sea otters.

FORAGING
SEAWEED SALAD

At the end of winter, **mountain goats** travel down to the intertidal zone to eat kelp. This helps them get the salt and minerals that are lacking in their diet.

UNIFORM
SEAWATER SWEATER

Northern sea otters spend much of their time floating on the water's surface in groups called rafts. They keep warm with the thickest fur in the world, with up to one million hairs per square inch.

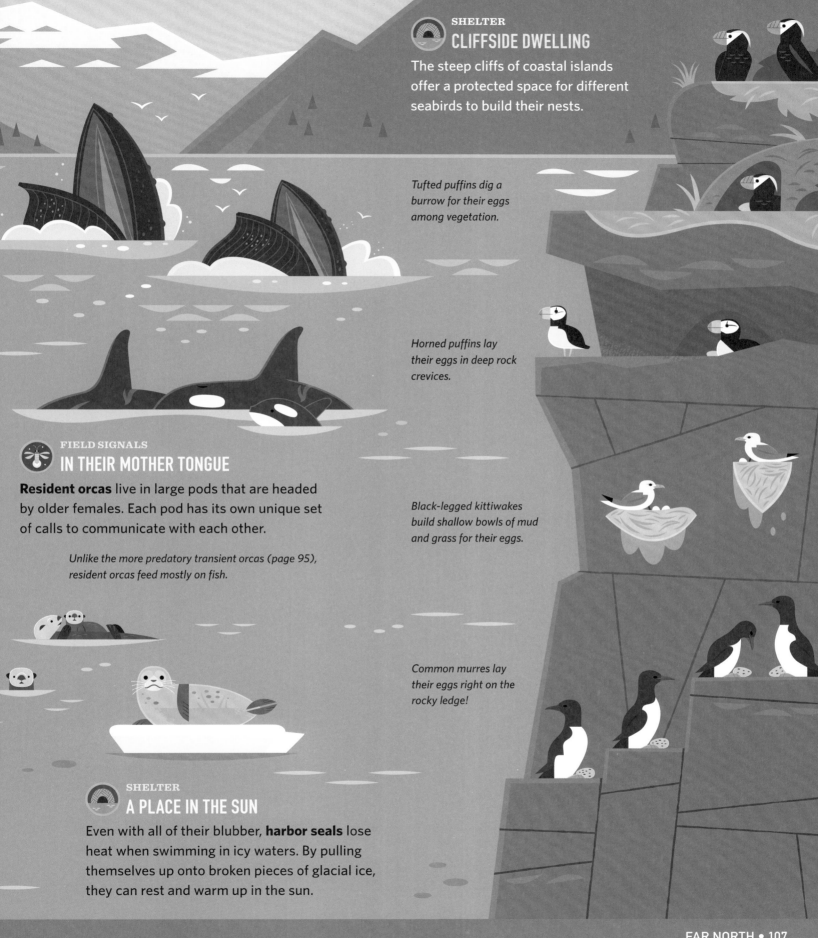

SHELTER

CLIFFSIDE DWELLING

The steep cliffs of coastal islands offer a protected space for different seabirds to build their nests.

Tufted puffins dig a burrow for their eggs among vegetation.

Horned puffins lay their eggs in deep rock crevices.

Black-legged kittiwakes build shallow bowls of mud and grass for their eggs.

Common murres lay their eggs right on the rocky ledge!

FIELD SIGNALS

IN THEIR MOTHER TONGUE

Resident orcas live in large pods that are headed by older females. Each pod has its own unique set of calls to communicate with each other.

Unlike the more predatory transient orcas (page 95), resident orcas feed mostly on fish.

SHELTER

A PLACE IN THE SUN

Even with all of their blubber, **harbor seals** lose heat when swimming in icy waters. By pulling themselves up onto broken pieces of glacial ice, they can rest and warm up in the sun.

THE NORTHERN FRONTIER

With more than 57 million acres of designated wilderness, Alaska has the largest intact natural landscapes in the United States. A rugged terrain of forested coastlines, dense taiga, and towering mountains leads to the vast, windswept tundra.

SHELTER
THE END OF THE JOURNEY

The **rufous hummingbird** ends its migration in southern Alaska, farther north than any other hummingbird. The female builds a nest high in a spruce or pine tree, using spiderwebs to hold it together and bits of lichen and moss to camouflage it.

To follow the rufous hummingbird on its migration, head to page 68.

FORAGING
A WINDSWEPT MEAL

In the winter, **Dall sheep** spend time on exposed mountainsides, where strong winds keep snow from piling too high on top of the lichens and frozen grasses they need to survive.

FORAGING
STICKY STORAGE

Canada jays don't migrate, so they survive the hardships of winter by using their saliva to stick bits of food under tree bark and on branches to eat later.

HUNTING
EXPANDED RANGE

Though only 2 feet long, the **American marten** will hunt across a territory of up to 15 square miles when food becomes scarce in the winter.

FORAGING
AN APPETITE FOR ANTLERS

North American porcupines are mostly herbivores but will eat bones and shed antlers to get extra sodium and calcium.

WILDERNESS EXPERTS
THE GULO GULO

The **wolverine** (also known as the *Gulo gulo*, **glutton**, or **skunk bear**) is well designed for life in the brutal north. Its extra-wide paws allow it to trek across snow, and its dense fur keeps it warm. With its strong sense of smell, it can locate carcasses up to 20 feet under the snow.

HUNTING
AN ALASKAN TASTING MENU

Gray wolves' ability to hunt for a wide variety of prey allows them to live in many different habitats across Alaska. They feed on moose and caribou in mainland Alaska, mountain goats and beavers in the southeast, and salmon and young seals along the coast.

TOOLKIT
BATTLE PADDLES

A bull **moose's** antlers, also called paddles, can stretch 6 feet across and weigh 40 pounds. Young bulls use their antlers to playfully spar with one another. As they grow older, the fights turn more dangerous as they battle one another for females or territory.

SEASONS OF THE TUNDRA

A treeless wilderness, the tundra is a region of two distinct seasons. Winters are harsh, with heavy snow and dark, cold nights. Over the brief summer, long days offer an opportunity for animals to stock up for the year.

rock ptarmigan

arctic fox

 UNIFORM
COAT CHANGE

Animals that don't migrate or hibernate must survive the long winter on the open tundra, where the lack of vegetation leaves them very exposed. Some of these animals survive by changing their coats, shedding the colors of summer for all-white winter camouflage.

snowshoe hare

 SHELTER
HOME FOR THE WINTER

Arctic ground squirrels spend eight months of every year hibernating in their underground burrows. Their body temperature can drop below freezing, lower than any other mammal.

 UNIFORM
A VERY HEAVY COAT

The insulated feathers of the **snowy owl** keep it warm and make it North America's heaviest owl: at an average of 4 pounds, it weighs twice as much as the taller great gray owl (page 62).

FORAGING
DIGGING UP DINNER

The long claws of the **grizzly** help it dig for grubs, roots, and burrowing rodents.

In the tough conditions of the tundra, grizzlies only grow to around 800 pounds.

In late summer, caribou begin to gather in herds to prepare for their migration.

rock ptarmigan

arctic fox

snowshoe hare

TOOLKIT
WING WARMERS

Arctic bumblebees can shiver their large flight muscles to heat themselves up.

FORAGING
A SUMMER FEAST

After **Arctic ground squirrels** emerge from their burrows in the summer, they have only a few months to eat enough grasses, seeds, and wildflowers to be able to survive the winter.

ACROSS THE EXPANSE

Western Alaska is a vast Arctic wilderness of tundra, rivers, and wetlands, roamed by herds of Ice Age mammals and visited by long-distance migrants from all over the world.

NAVIGATION
FROM AROUND THE GLOBE

In the summer, millions of birds return from wintering grounds all over the world to nest in western Alaska.

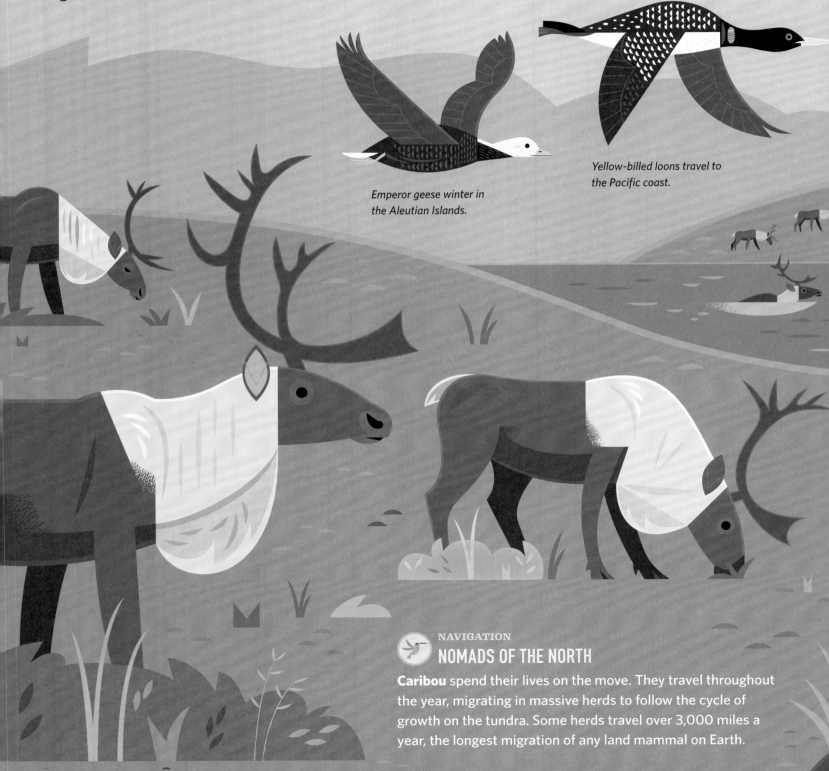

Emperor geese winter in the Aleutian Islands.

Yellow-billed loons travel to the Pacific coast.

NAVIGATION
NOMADS OF THE NORTH

Caribou spend their lives on the move. They travel throughout the year, migrating in massive herds to follow the cycle of growth on the tundra. Some herds travel over 3,000 miles a year, the longest migration of any land mammal on Earth.

Pacific golden plovers migrate to islands throughout the Pacific, including Hawai'i.

Long-tailed jaegers spend the other half of the year south of the equator.

Northern wheatears winter in North Africa.

Bar-tailed godwits travel from Alaska to New Zealand in one nonstop 7,000-mile flight.

Arctic warblers winter among the islands of Southeast Asia.

Arctic terns migrate to Antarctica, flying farther than any other bird.

Caribou are strong swimmers, able to cross wide, rushing rivers.

COMMUNITY
LINE OF DEFENSE

Musk oxen live in herds headed by a female leader. If the herd is approached by a predator, they line up to form a barrier. If there are multiple predators, they form a circle around their young, protecting them from all angles.

sandhill cranes

tundra swan

bristle-thighed curlew

FROZEN SEAS

For the wildlife of Alaska's seas, life follows a cycle of freezing and thawing. In the winter, "fast ice" connects to the shore, creating a frozen plain over the water. This melts in the summer, leaving only isolated outposts of floating "pack ice." As ocean temperatures rise, this delicate rhythm is increasingly threatened.

UNIFORM
AN INSULATED WETSUIT

Bowhead whales are particularly well adapted to living in icy waters. They have the thickest blubber in the world, up to 1.5 feet thick in places!

NAVIGATION
GOING THEIR SEPARATE WAYS

In the winter, **Pacific walruses** gather on pack ice in the Bering Sea to mate. In the spring, females leave the males and follow the receding ice north. Along their journey, the females who were impregnated the previous winter give birth on ice floes. They'll spend the warmer months safely isolated on the remote pack ice of the Chukchi Sea, hunting in shallow waters, socializing, and caring for their young.

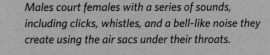

Males court females with a series of sounds, including clicks, whistles, and a bell-like noise they create using the air sacs under their throats.

HUNTING
THE SPOILS OF WINTER

Unlike for many animals, winter is a time of richness for the **polar bear**. Most polar bears travel out onto the frozen fast ice, where they fatten up on the blubber of seals, walruses, and beluga whales. The weight they gain over winter must sustain them through the summer, when they'll return to shore to survive on less nutrient-rich foods, like roots, berries, and eggs.

Arctic foxes follow polar bears across the ice, hoping to scavenge on the remains of their hunts.

FIELD SIGNALS
CANARIES OF THE SEA

Beluga whales make a steady chatter of clicks, chirps, and whistles. Communicating with sound is particularly useful in the long, dark winter nights.

UNIFORM
A SPOTLESS COAT

Spotted seal pups spend their first few weeks on the ice, where their white fur helps them camouflage. They molt into their spotted coats when they're ready to start diving.

Male walrus use their tusks to fight for dominance.

ISLANDS OF THE PACIFIC

Volcanic activity has created mountains and islands all around the Pacific Ocean, including two very different archipelagos in the United States: the Aleutian Islands and the Hawaiian Islands.

Laysan albatross

gray whale

whiskered auklets

crested auklets

THE ALEUTIAN ISLANDS

Extending 1,200 miles from the Alaska Peninsula across the northern Pacific, the Aleutian Islands are a rich maritime habitat for seabirds and marine mammals.

 ATHLETICS
DEEP DIVES

King eider forage nearly 200 feet deep for mollusks and starfish, while **ribbon seals** dive almost 2,000 feet to hunt for pollock and cod. **Elephant seals** have been recorded pursuing squid and octopus at depths of over 5,000 feet!

 HUNTING
CHILLED JELLY

Leatherback sea turtles feed on jellyfish off the coast of Alaska. Their large body generates its own heat, helping them swim in colder water than any other sea turtle can.

lion's mane jellyfish

 COMMUNITY
DEEP-SEA GARDENS

In the icy waters off the Aleutians is an unexpected animal community: deep sea **coral**. Over 100 species of coral thrive here, including many found nowhere else on Earth.

THE HAWAIIAN ISLANDS

Twenty-four thousand miles south of the Aleutians lies the most isolated archipelago in the world: the Hawaiian Islands. Despite their seclusion, they're visited annually by marine migrants from all across the Pacific Ocean.

 ATHLETICS
A COLOSSAL BATTLE

After spending the summer feeding off the coast of Alaska (page 106), **humpback whales** travel 3,000 miles to their mating grounds in Hawai'i. When a female signals that she's ready to mate, it kicks off an epic underwater battle between the males for her attention. They collide at high speeds, even jumping out of the water to land atop their rivals.

 HUNTING
PACIFIC HUNTING GROUNDS

Great white sharks summer off the coast of California (page 95) but spend the winter in the open ocean, where they feed on deep-sea creatures. Some make it as far west as Hawai'i, where they hunt in coastal waters.

 NAVIGATION
EN ROUTE

Hawai'i is only a stopping point for **leatherback sea turtles** on their journey to Indonesia, where they'll lay their eggs. They make one of the longest migrations in the world: over 10,000 miles.

 FORAGING
DOING SOMERAULTS

Giant manta rays will sometimes engage in barrel rolling to sweep up zooplankton.

BELOW THE WAVES

The Hawaiian Islands are surrounded by vast stretches of deep, open ocean in all directions. Closer to shore, animals thrive in the warmer waters of sheltered lagoons, shallow channels, and coral reefs.

UNIFORM

TWO-TONE CAMOUFLAGE

Like many other ocean hunters, the **manō kihikihi (hammerhead shark)** has coloration known as counter-shading. Its top half is dark, so it can blend in with the water when seen from above, and its underside is nearly white, so it disappears in the light when seen from below.

HUNTING

TO THE DEPTHS OF THE SEA

The **ʻIlioholoikauaua (Hawaiian monk seal)** dives to depths of over 1,000 feet to hunt for squid along the sea floor.

NAVIGATION

INTERNAL COMPASS

The **hihimanu (spotted eagle ray)** migrates by using sensory pores that help it detect Earth's magnetic field.

FORAGING

NOSY EATERS

The **honuʻea (Hawaiian hawksbill turtle)** uses its narrow beak to feed on sponges, while the **lau-wiliwili-nukunukuʻoiʻoi (longnose butterflyfish)** probes for food in coral and in rocky crevices using its long, thin snout.

ATHLETICS
THE FLYING FISH

To get away from predators, the **mālolo (flying fish)** propels itself out of the water, gliding for hundreds of feet on its wing-like fins.

COMMUNITY
TURTLE WASH

Honu (the **Hawaiian green sea turtle**) regularly visits reefs, where it knows local fish will help clean it of algae and parasites. The fish get a meal, and the turtle will be able to swim more easily with a cleaner shell.

black surgeonfish

yellow tang

TOOLKIT
HARD TO SWALLOW

To avoid being eaten, the **kokala (porcupine fish)** fills its expandable stomach with water, inflating its body and extending the sharp spines that cover its body.

TOOLKIT
HAWAIIAN TROPIC

The **Hawaiian whitespotted toby** creates its own sunscreen-like substance to protect itself from the sun.

UNIFORM
LITTLE RED HIDING FISH

The brilliant red coloring of the **'ala'ihi (Hawaiian squirrelfish)** actually helps it hide from predators, because red is the first color to disappear from the color spectrum underwater.

UNIFORM
SAFETY STRIPES

The high-contrast stripes on the **kihikihi (Moorish idol)** make it harder for predators to tell where the fish starts and where it ends.

HUNTING
SCENT TRACKING

The **puhi kauila (dragon moray eel)** has long nostril tubes, which help it follow scents as it hunts through coral reefs.

SHELTERING SHORES

Hawai'i is made up of over 130 islands, ranging from the 4,000-square-mile "Big Island" to islets that are little more than a patch of open sand. Their isolation in the Pacific makes them a valuable refuge for animals hauling out from the surrounding seas or arriving from around the globe.

gray-backed tern

 **NAVIGATION**
A LIFE AT SEA

Pelagic birds spend most of the year hunting the ocean, often only coming ashore to nest. The remoteness of Hawai'i makes it an ideal nursery, so every year millions of seabirds cross the Pacific to breed on islands throughout the archipelago.

Hawaiian petrel

Laysan albatross nest on the Northern Hawaiian Islands but soar thousands of miles across the ocean to hunt for squid. Glide to pages 97 and 116 to see where they travel.

 PERFORMANCE
THE ALBATROSS COTILLION

Long-lived birds, **mōlī (laysan albatross)** don't mate until they are seven or more years old. To select a partner, they perform a courtship dance in which they bow, shake their heads, and preen one another. The moves take practice to get right, but once they're bonded, they'll mate for life.

 ATHLETICS
SKIPPING ROCK POOLS

Pāo`o (zebra blennies) live in rock pools along the high-tide line. Though they may seem trapped when the tide recedes, they can leap from one pool to another to evade predators.

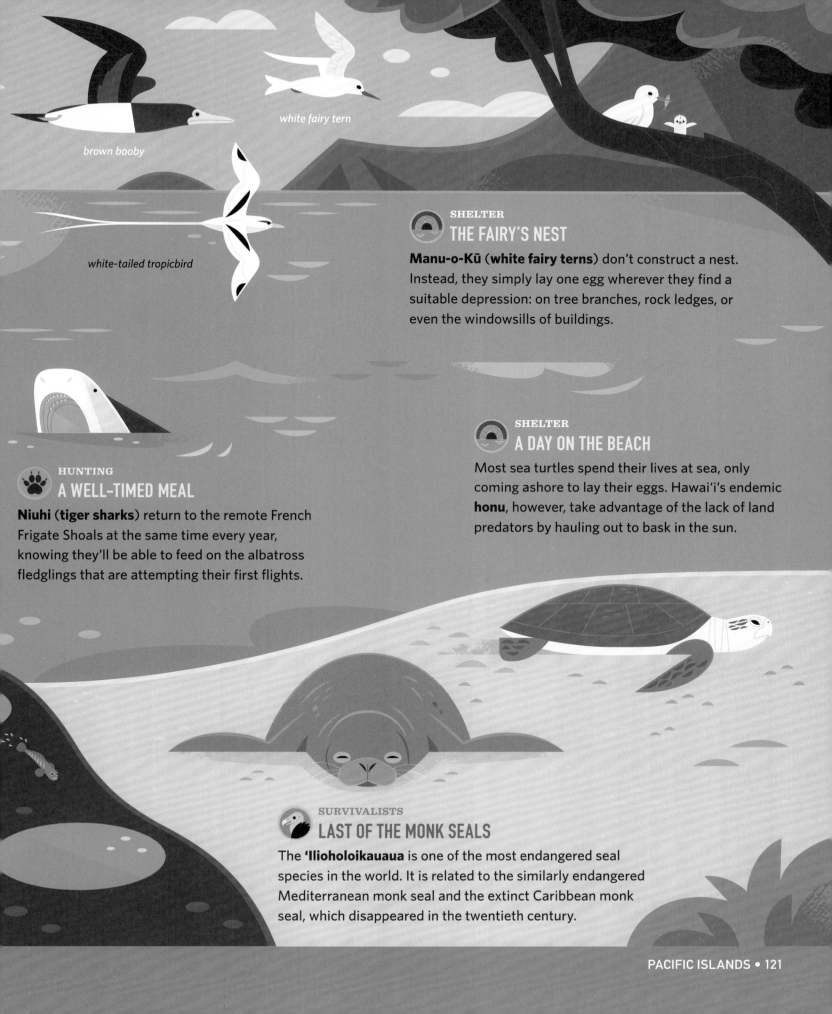

brown booby

white fairy tern

white-tailed tropicbird

SHELTER
THE FAIRY'S NEST

Manu-o-Kū (white fairy terns) don't construct a nest. Instead, they simply lay one egg wherever they find a suitable depression: on tree branches, rock ledges, or even the windowsills of buildings.

HUNTING
A WELL-TIMED MEAL

Niuhi (tiger sharks) return to the remote French Frigate Shoals at the same time every year, knowing they'll be able to feed on the albatross fledglings that are attempting their first flights.

SHELTER
A DAY ON THE BEACH

Most sea turtles spend their lives at sea, only coming ashore to lay their eggs. Hawai'i's endemic **honu**, however, take advantage of the lack of land predators by hauling out to bask in the sun.

SURVIVALISTS
LAST OF THE MONK SEALS

The **'Ilioholoikauaua** is one of the most endangered seal species in the world. It is related to the similarly endangered Mediterranean monk seal and the extinct Caribbean monk seal, which disappeared in the twentieth century.

ISLAND LIFE

Created by undersea volcanoes, the islands of Hawai'i have never been connected to a continental landmass, so all wildlife had to arrive by sea or air. Once on the islands, animals evolved to fit the unique challenges and opportunities they were given, some developing unusual practices or unique physical forms.

SHELTER
THE BURROWING BIRD

The **'ua'u** (**Hawaiian petrel**) spends most of its time at sea, but it comes ashore to nest. It lays its eggs in underground burrows, preferring remote habitats, like the alpine slopes of the Mauna Loa volcano or the cliffs of Waimea Canyon.

TOOLKIT
BIRDBRAINED

One of the only tool-using birds in the world, the highly intelligent **'alalā** (**Hawaiian crow**) will use sticks to extract insects from rotting trees or logs.

The Hawaiian crow was declared extinct in the wild in 2002, but conservationists are working to help them recover.

TOOLKIT
LAVA BOOTS

Even when hardened, lava is dangerous to walk on: it's jagged, and it breaks easily. The **nēnē** (**Hawaiian goose**) has tough feet with less webbing than other geese, which helps it walk across lava rocks as it searches for food.

A close relative of the Canada goose (page 36), the nēnē likely evolved from geese that arrived in Hawai'i 500,000 years ago.

TOOLKIT
SUCTION CUPS

O'opu (**Hawaiian goby**) migrate from the ocean to freshwater to lay their eggs. To reach the remote streams and pools where they'll breed, some species of o'opu must scale towering waterfalls, gripping the wet rock surface using the same suckers that they use to eat algae. They've been recorded climbing hundreds of feet!

UNIFORM
DIFFERENT PLACES, DIFFERENT FACES

Groups of **nananana makaki'i** (**happy face spiders**) that live in isolation from one another have very different markings and may be in the process of evolving into several unique species.

HUNTING
CARNIVOROUS CATERPILLARS

Caterpillars generally feed on vegetation, but most of Hawai'i's **eupithecia caterpillars** capture and eat other insects.

PERFORMANCE
FLIES OF PARADISE

Fruit flies have evolved into hundreds of different species on the Hawaiian Islands, many of which perform their own unique courtship displays. In some species, males will even battle for territory.

TOOLKIT
HONEYCREEPERS

Relatives of the finch, **Hawaiian honeycreepers** have evolved uniquely shaped beaks, which allow them to pursue many different sources of food.

The 'akiapōlā'au uses its bill to peck open tree bark and pull out insects.

The Maui 'alauahio uses its small beak to flip over lichen in search of insects.

The long, curved beak of the 'i'iwi lets it drink nectar from inside deep flowers.

The crossbill of the 'akepa helps it pull caterpillars out of buds.

ACROSS THE PACIFIC

Nearly on the other side of the world from mainland United States, the territories of Guam, American Samoa, and the Northern Mariana Islands are home to their own unique creatures.

Samoa flying fox

FORAGING
THE FRUIT DOVE

True to its name, the **Mariana fruit dove** feeds on fruit in the forest canopy, particularly figs.

FORAGING
THE GARDENING BAT

By feeding on fruit, **flying foxes** help pollinate plants and spread seeds throughout the forest.

SHELTER
A MEGA NEST

Micronesian megapodes bury their eggs in enormous mounds of soil and vegetation, which can measure up to 8 feet across.

SURVIVALISTS
THE RELOCATED RAIL

The flightless **ko'ko'** (**Guam rail**) was hunted to extinction in the wild by invasive brown tree snakes. The nearby island of Rota is snake-free, so ko'ko' were relocated there to build a breeding colony.

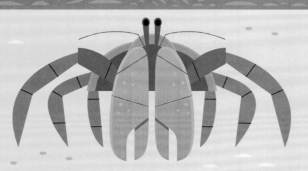

TOOLKIT
SMELL DETECTORS

Since the **Samoan coconut crab** lives on land and not in the water, its antennae are specially suited to pick up smells in the air.

The Samoan coconut crab can have a leg span of up to 30 inches!

UNIFORM
WATERPROOF SUNSCREEN

The bold colors of **giant clams** may help protect them from getting damaged by the bright tropical sun.

FORAGING
LANDSCAPE MAINTENANCE

Convict surgeonfish graze on the algae that grows on coral, which helps keep the coral healthy.

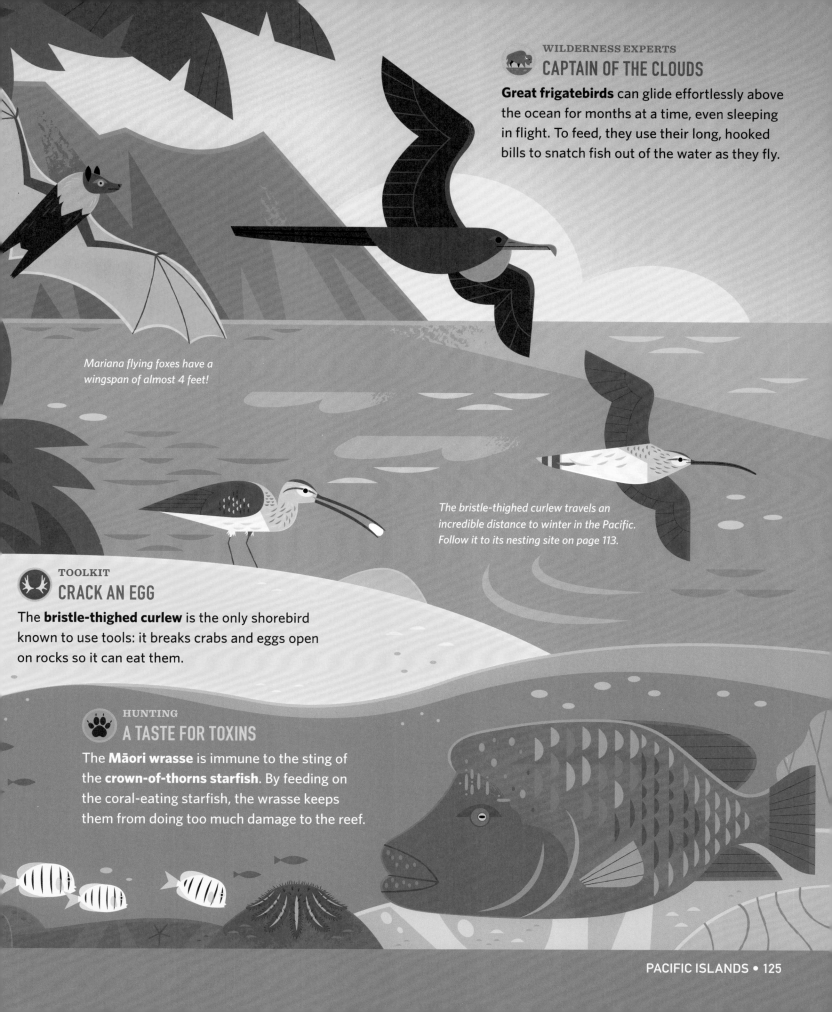

WILDERNESS EXPERTS
CAPTAIN OF THE CLOUDS

Great frigatebirds can glide effortlessly above the ocean for months at a time, even sleeping in flight. To feed, they use their long, hooked bills to snatch fish out of the water as they fly.

Mariana flying foxes have a wingspan of almost 4 feet!

The bristle-thighed curlew travels an incredible distance to winter in the Pacific. Follow it to its nesting site on page 113.

TOOLKIT
CRACK AN EGG

The **bristle-thighed curlew** is the only shorebird known to use tools: it breaks crabs and eggs open on rocks so it can eat them.

HUNTING
A TASTE FOR TOXINS

The **Māori wrasse** is immune to the sting of the **crown-of-thorns starfish**. By feeding on the coral-eating starfish, the wrasse keeps them from doing too much damage to the reef.

INDEX

AUTHOR'S NOTE

Early in my childhood I entered an animal phase that I have yet to grow out of.

I grew up in New Mexico, spending my summers at day camps hosted by my local zoo and natural history museum, getting ever more drawn into an obsession with the natural world. At the time, it seemed without question that my interest in animals and wild spaces was also an interest in the world outside of the United States. I became more and more curious about the grasslands of Africa, the islands of Southeast Asia, and the rainforests of South America, places where to my young mind, the natural world seemed truly "wild."

As a young adult I was able to pursue this interest by moving abroad, first to South Africa and then to Thailand and Taiwan. I traveled and got outdoors as often as I could, seeing places I had dreamed of in my childhood.

I returned to the United States to study illustration at the Art Center College of Design in Pasadena, CA, and despite it being a return to my home country, it was as though I were seeing its wild spaces for the first time. Surreal desert gardens, where life flourished among towering saguaros; subtropical swamps, prowled by predators from the age of the dinosaurs; and fog-cloaked Pacific forests, where rare seabirds and endangered condors nested in the tallest trees on Earth. I came to realize that of all the wild spaces I had explored, the wildest had been right where my journey had begun.

Since starting this project, my days have been spent reading books on grizzlies and wolves, paging through academic reports on prairie dog burrows, and spending at least two hours a week on bird-watching websites. However, I've learned the most when I've been able to escape the studio and get outdoors, even just for a hike in my neighborhood or a quick trip to see the herons nesting at my local reservoir.

In sharing what I've learned, I hope that this book will be a call to action for anyone who reads it. The animals we share this land with are incredible, unique, strange, and beautiful, but they are also very vulnerable to our actions. Pollution, habitat loss, and climate change are imperiling our natural spaces and threatening our wild neighbors like never before. I hope you will join me in working together to do everything we can to preserve and protect them.

ALEXANDER VIDAL

First draft written by lantern light,
beneath the redwoods at Big Basin State Park, CA
September 14th, 2019